HOW TO
FRAME
YOUR OWN
PICTURES

For Bea and Willem, my two creative sparks
With special thanks to Andrew Edson, and Roze, John, George,
William and Oliver Sherwood

'Tools ... A link with our past, the human past, the hand'
American pop artist Jim Dine, whose parents owned a hardware store.

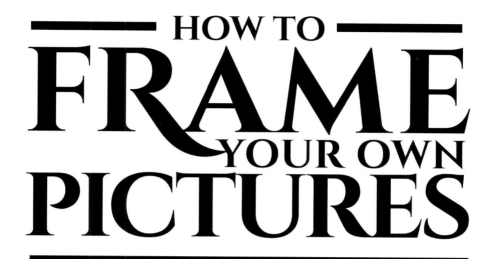

HOW TO
FRAME
YOUR OWN
PICTURES

JANE WARREN

WHITE OWL
AN IMPRINT OF PEN & SWORD BOOKS LTD.
YORKSHIRE – PHILADELPHIA

First published in Great Britain in 2021 by
Pen & Sword WHITE OWL
An imprint of
Pen & Sword Books Ltd
Yorkshire – Philadelphia

Copyright © Jane Warren 2021

ISBN 9781526775719

Printed and bound in India by Replika Press Pvt. Ltd.

Photographs by Bea Mulder and Jane Warren
Design: Paul Wilkinson

Pen & Sword Books Limited incorporates the imprints of Atlas, Archaeology, Aviation, Discovery, Family History, Fiction, History, Maritime, Military, Military Classics, Politics, Select, Transport, True Crime, Air World, Frontline Publishing, Leo Cooper, Remember When, Seaforth Publishing, The Praetorian Press, Wharncliffe Local History, Wharncliffe Transport, Wharncliffe True Crime and White Owl.

For a complete list of Pen & Sword titles please contact:
PEN & SWORD BOOKS LIMITED
47 Church Street, Barnsley, South Yorkshire, S70 2AS, England
E-mail: enquiries@pen-and-sword.co.uk
Website: www.pen-and-sword.co.uk

Or
PEN AND SWORD BOOKS
1950 Lawrence Rd, Havertown, PA 19083, USA
E-mail: Uspen-and-sword@casematepublishers.com
Website: www.penandswordbooks.com

CONTENTS

INTRODUCTION TO EASY DIY FRAMING

PICTURE FRAMES ARE both protective and decorative – and definitely very satisfying to create. When my son started school in 2009, I set up a picture-framing micro-business from a studio in my woodland garden in West Sussex. I called it Woodland Pie because it seems to me that making a picture frame is a bit like making a pie – a series of satisfying small steps, but not too much of any one stage. I think this makes it fun. It also means you can make a frame pretty quickly, once you have done it a few times.

I've always enjoyed hobby framing having undertaken a brilliant short course in 2002 at the wonderful West Dean College in West Sussex, between writing assignments. Since then, I've developed my skills and done quite a lot of experimentation. I believe that framing should be creatively expressive, rather than an exercise in military precision. So I'll also show you fudges and fixes to keep that positive energy flowing. Every frame is different and no frame has to be perfect; just 'good enough' – I'd certainly have appreciated a framing book that was a bit more relaxed and organic when I was experimenting with this rewarding craft.

As well as eight bespoke projects, I reveal my tried and trusted shortcuts to making something rather more long lasting than a pie, showing how you too can discover the satisfaction of showcasing treasures – as well as creating framed gifts – on a budget.

Even if you have no previous knowledge of framing, you'll learn simple techniques and discover how investing in a few essential hand tools and basic materials can save hundreds of pounds on your framing costs while helping you create high-quality handmade gifts for family and friends (if you feel like sharing).

Using my step-by-step instructions and easy-to-follow techniques, as well as 'insider tips', you'll be able to get started quickly on a wide variety of enjoyable projects.

The Woodland Pie framing style is all about creating: making easy, attractive and artistic frames from basic timber and always using hand-painted or handmade finishes.

I really don't like most of the expensive (and dull) factory-finished timber mouldings you find in picture framing shops (and most picture framing instruction books), especially when the possibilities for decorating your own frames can easily – and inexpensively – transform bare timber into any manner of finishes, including gold leaf, black enamel (good for photographic prints), a colourful distressed look, copper embossed metal or decoupage.

Watch out for my 'insider tip' on how to create a lustrous, versatile, 'go-to' paint effect using nothing other than leftover household emulsion paint, water, and wire wool!

In my experience, picture framing books also usually include far too much information, which can be off-putting. So I've set about writing an accessible how-to book, not a picture framing encyclopedia. It aims to cut out the unnecessary, and get you hobby framing in no time – with flair and creativity.

First, I'll introduce you to the small palette of affordable materials and hand tools you really need – and won't ask you to invest in anything non-essential. I can't bear equipment lists that go on and on and make you think, 'Really? Do I need all this to do that?' – putting you off before you've even started.

You'll find plenty of step-by-step-photos of techniques – including mount cutting and the foolproof way to make strong corner joints – and I've also taken pains to describe each step quite carefully. I'm going to assume

WHY FRAME?

Frames are utilitarian works of craft, but they don't have to be purely functional. While a glazed frame has an important practical function – protecting delicate artwork such as watercolours or line drawings from moisture and dust – they also lend atmosphere to a work of art (or photograph) and amplify the message they are sending. You only have to think of a majestic oil painting in an elaborate gilded frame, or a black and white snap in a contemporary black box frame – with crisp white mount – to appreciate all the good PR that frames give the images they showcase.

IT WASN'T UNTIL the Florentine Renaissance of the early fifteenth century, that the idea of frames for pictures was born. Before then, most Italian artists painted on elaborate wooden panels which were covered in a layer of linen pasted on to the hidden timber sub-structure. But in 1423, a banker named Palla Strozzi – the richest man in Florence – commissioned Gentile da Fabriano to paint a religious panel painting with a gilded frame surrounding it. This unleashed the creativity of Florentine woodworkers. Drawing from classical architecture and the decorative vocabulary they already used in carving panels and chests, they began to produce ever more elaborate decorative frames. But while painters earned fame and fortune for their artistic works, the highly skilled frame makers remained largely anonymous – as they do today.

A photograph of my daughter's desk displayed in an elaborate vintage gilded frame; a light-hearted pairing which suggests the importance of childhood creativity. It also shows the impact an ornate frame can make.

you have no prior woodworking know-how, so each step will be explained in simple language that will get you framing in no time. I suggest reading the 'recipe' in each chapter thoroughly from top to bottom, before embarking. That old builders' adage: 'Measure twice: Cut once' will be your best friend when using this book.

My eight featured projects showcase a variety of styles and ideas, from simple box frames using readily available cheap pine lengths of different dimensions, to stretching canvas artwork over an easy-to-make frame that doesn't require a single angled 'mitre' joint. Another project will show you how to make a shadow 'memory' box for a three-dimensional object or collection. You will learn how to make a mirror from rough-sawn planks, and a simple cork, chalk or peg board using decoupage. I'll also show you how to try your hand at embossing and gilding more unusual frames.

In the Resources section you can discover where to buy must-have tools and materials.

To get started, take a look at an unframed picture and ask yourself 'what do I like best about this image, and how can I enhance that?'

The rest is as easy as pie.

A NOTE ABOUT THE PHOTOGRAPHY

I usually photograph my finished frames by hanging them against trees in our oak and hazel copse, often with a tendril of ivy or honeysuckle against the painted woodwork. Frame photography can be very dry, but photographer Bea Mulder has helped to capture each project in a natural setting. She also drew the illustrations in the introductory chapter.

Jane Warren, West Sussex

IDEAS FOR INSPIRATION

PICTURE FRAMING IS a win-win (or possibly a win-win-win). After all, the process is enormously enjoyable, and you are engaged in a productive craft that also saves you money. Everyone has a to-be-framed pile and I've been lucky enough to make a wide variety of frames for friends, family and clients. Hopefully the images on these pages will give you some ideas for your own framing projects.

The colour of the frame, the width of mount around the image, as well as the style of frame itself – whether contemporary, traditional, or something else entirely – all enhance the viewer's relationship with the showcased image. The artwork is the focal point, and the frame should always flatter and enhance it.

A fun friend asked me to give her young son's self-portrait the gallery treatment – I upcycled an old frame with gold paint, and stretched vintage velvet over the mount.

A beautiful embroidery by a friend's daughter which I was asked to float-mount as a birthday surprise.

A box frame is a wonderful way to reunite man and medals, I gave the frame a slightly aged look to reflect the time since the conflict in which he served.

A box frame with a delicate hand-painted gold bevel.

A box frame and floating mount for this confident salamander painted on board by a client's child.

A twin pair of matching frames can be very eye-catching, as with this Asian artwork.

A simple gold-painted box frame to draw attention to the striking Chinese image it showcases.

A wide mount for this street scene from Tangiers, Morocco, painted by my mother Susan in the 1960s. The dark grey frame is colour-matched by eye to the shadow under the archway to draw your eye into the image.

It's wonderful going all out on colour as with the crimson that picks out the tail feathers of this sassy bird.

Two birds in colours to highlight and accentuate their plumage.

Applying two coats of emulsion and rubbing with sandpaper creates a pleasing distressed look.

Be bold with colour as in this large glazed frame highlighting the regal nature of this vintage map in ruby red and gold.

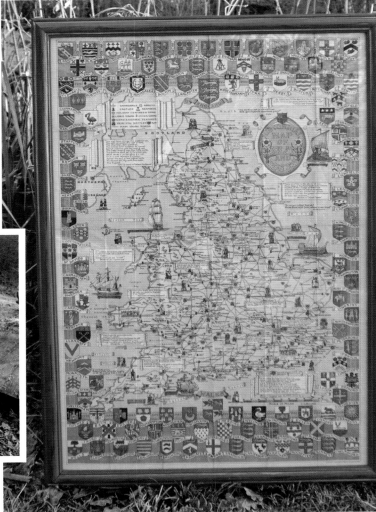

Framing a favourite piece of children's artwork is a cherished memory.

Because this Asian cartoon was already cropped to the top of the canvas, I cut a narrower margin at the top of the mount board to help make visual sense of it. I picked out the yellow as it was the least dominant colour in the screen print.

Hand-painted and buffed emulsion finish with contrasting top coat.

Highlighting the edges of the frame can be fun as in this knock-off Andy Warhol painted by a friend.

I sandpapered this two-tone frame back to the bare wood to give a vintage feel to this lovely child's drawing.

I used gold leaf to contrast with the simple beads on these South African necklaces that were given to my Aunty Rosemary when she lived there as a little girl. They had lain in tissue paper for many decades.

In these companion box frames – the puzzle and the solution – I stretched grey fabric over the mount before framing to give a lustrous setting to the Picasso plates.

Photography doesn't always need a mount to create an arresting image, as this vintage frame treatment for my daughter's self-portrait proves. The contrast with the setting is equally striking.

The colour of the frame changes our relationship with the contents. These would have looked dramatically different in green-painted frames.

The frame picks out the rich colours of the distant sea and the purple flowers 'pop' as a consequence, but I think this may have been more effective had the frame been a muted grey.

This simple frame was uplifted by a hand-painted two-tone buffed finish on the wide moulding.

This was a big frame for a friend's Ordnance Survey map from which she can plot the walks in Sussex countryside that she loves.

Unglazed box frame made for a local artist.

Unglazed box frame made for an artist's exhibition, painted in contrasting black for impact.

Up-cycling an old frame with a coat of gold paint for a new lease of life.

MUST-HAVE TOOLS AND MATERIALS

I FIND THE days I spend in my picture framing studio, amidst the oak and hazel trees in our woodland garden, to be among the most emotionally nourishing I know. Using your hands to make something meaningful or beautiful into a permanent memory that can be hung on a wall for lifelong enjoyment is satisfying on so many levels.

Like any craft, the ease and enjoyment of picture framing is all about having the right equipment. Here is my must-have list of picture framing essentials. I promise you won't need anything else.

1. Vintage corner clamp.
2. Modern corner clamp.
3. Set square.
4. Metal ruler.
5. Mount cutter.
6. Straight edge.

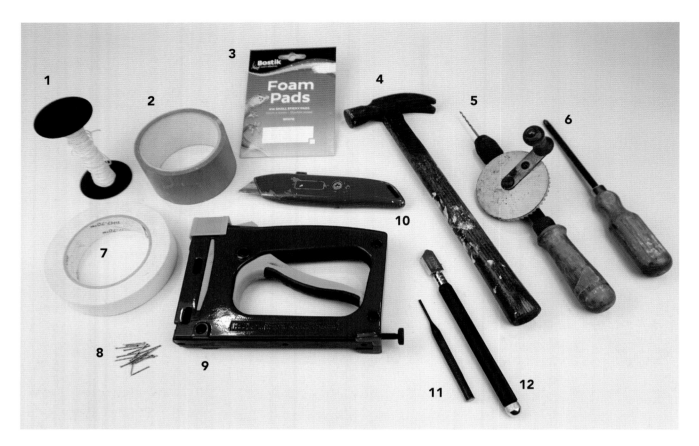

1. **Picture framing cord. 2. Brown tape. 3. Self-adhesive foam pads. 4. Hammer. 5. Hand drill with 2mm drill bit (optional). 6. Cross-head screwdriver. 7. Acid-free mount tape/masking tape. 8. Panel pins. 9. Point driver gun (optional). 10. Stanley knife. 11. Bradawl (if you don't have a hand drill). 12. Glass-cutter (optional).**

1. **Hanging straps for heavy frames.**
2. **9mm wood screws.**
3. **D rings.**
4. **Everbuild waterproof wood adhesive.**
5. **Polyvine decorators varnish.**
6. **Danish oil.**
7. **Mod podge sealer.**
8. **¾" sash brush.**
9. **Basic brush.**
10. **Artist's brush for fine detail.**

Hand tools are easy to use, rarely go wrong, and are portable and affordable. They are also aesthetically enjoyable to work with: definitely the 'slow food' approach to picture-framing. It's satisfying to work quietly, using a little muscle power and ingenuity to frame your treasures, while Radio 4 (or whatever) burbles away in the background.

EQUIPMENT:

Mitre Saw

A mitre saw is one of the big secrets behind a professionally framed picture. For the cost of having one picture framed, this excellent piece of equipment will enable you to frame dozens of pictures yourself.

Set the mitre saw blade to the marked 45-degree angle by moving it to the left or right, depending which end of the timber you are cutting. The saw is held in a guide rail that enables you to cut your chosen angle in your moulding with ease. (A moulding is a piece of wood with an interesting profile and an overhanging lip or 'rebate' to hold the frame contents in place.)

Once your timber is in position, secure it by tightening the threaded rubber-ended clamp on the front of the mitre saw. Hold the timber steady with your hand, and use your other hand to grasp the saw handle and move the blade vigorously back and forth. This will enable you to cut an angled piece from your chosen moulding. This will take around 20–40 seconds per cut.

Cutting two opposing 45-degree angles on four timber pieces enables them to be securely attached together to form the four corners of your frame.

The one 'consumable' part of a mitre saw is the saw blade (easily available online for a few pounds). It's unlikely to need replacing until you've made a couple of dozen frames, as each cut is so small. You'll know it's time to replace when it takes twice as long as usual to saw your timber.

Corner Clamp

After you have cut four timber mouldings, each with two angled ends, you will need to attach them together to form the frame. This is done using wood glue (which makes a joint as strong as the wood

INSIDER TIP:
Consider using clamps to hold your mitre saw on to the work surface to stop it moving around and wasting your energy. Alternatively, mount it on a short wooden plank, and drill two 8mm-wide holes through the plank and all the way through the work surface underneath (if not using your kitchen table!). Whenever you are using your mitre saw, these holes will enable you to secure it to the work surface with long threaded bolts and wing nuts, which are easy to tighten and undo.

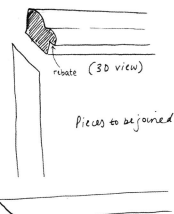

Mitre join

rebate (3D view)

Pieces to be joined

mitre joint

itself when dry) and slender nails known as panel pins.

The secret to a professional-looking frame is a tight mitre joint on each of the four corners. This is achieved by using a picture-framing corner clamp to keep the two pieces of timber in position while you fix their angled ends together, corner by corner.

A mitre joint is made by cutting two pieces of timber at a 45-degree angle and connecting them together to form a 90-degree corner when they are joined together.

My vintage mitre clamp was bought by 1970s football pundit Jimmy Hill for his novelist wife Bryony. She gave it to me two decades ago when I went to their home to interview her about her latest novel, and explained that Jimmy had brought it back for her from the US during her brief framing flirtation. Shame she didn't have this book! Anyway, it remains a joy to use.

Mount board cutter

Another trade secret for a professional-looking frame is a bevel-edge mount board cutter. It enables you to easily cut out the 'aperture' in your mount – the inner square or rectangle behind which you will affix your photograph or artwork. The 45-degree bevel edge that it creates – revealing the core of the cardboard mount – confers instant polish.

The cutter should be used with a ruler. The more expensive cutters have a locating lug that glides easily along a companion 'straight edge' for more accurate cutting – indispensable, really, for larger frames.

When cutting out the aperture in a mount, keep a steady pressure on the straight edge (or ruler) with your left hand, while pushing the cutter with your right hand (some cutters cut by pulling rather than pushing). The secret is to press down very firmly on the straight edge or ruler so that it does not move around while you are cutting. It may take a little bit of practice to avoid wonky cuts, so experiment on some offcuts of mount board first.

You will need a pack of replaceable blades to ensure crisp cuts in your mount, as cardboard can blunt them quite quickly.

Stanley knife or disposable craft knives

Used for cutting the outside edges of your mount, backing board and Art Bak board, as well as the brown self-adhesive framing tape on the back of the frame that keeps out dust. You will need a pack of replacement blades for a Stanley knife.

Hammer

To tap in the panel pins on the corners of the frame.

Punch

Used with the hammer to tap the tips of the panel pins beneath the surface of the timber by 1–2mm. This enables the tiny holes to be filled with wood filler (or wood glue and sawdust) and sanded smooth before painting.

Long ruler (approx. 60cm)

Really useful for measuring mount board and Art Bak board accurately, although a tape measure will also work if you measure carefully.

Set square

This is a useful item for drawing right angles on mount board and Art Bak board prior to cutting them out.

INSIDER TIP:
Make your own DIY set square by cutting a large corner off the edge of a piece of mount board (longer side; shorter bottom). Level up with the bottom edge of the mount, and use a pencil to draw a vertical line prior to cutting the mount board for your frame.

Hand drill and 2–3mm timber drill bit

Used to make small pilot holes for fixing the screws used for the D-rings on the back of the frame, and for the panel pins during frame assembly. If you don't have a drill, a bradawl will also work – this small sharp tool is used to make an indentation in timber to enable screws or pins to be fitted with ease.

Cross-head screwdriver
For securing D-rings to the back of the frame with small cross-head screws.

Paint brush
For decorating your frame. Any small paint brush will do, but it's worth investing around £4 on a ¾in wide 'sash' window brush from a local hardware store. These hold a lot of paint but taper to a point for precision, and their soft bristles don't leave streak marks.

Steel wool
This comes in different grades. You will need 0000 to create the easy lustrous buffed finish I recommend on Page 38-40. Pull off an apricot-sized piece and squash into a small pad. Use until it disintegrates, and replace.

Saw or hacksaw
Only a handful of projects in the book require you to cut hardboard or timber with a conventional saw, so check your chosen project before buying one.

Cutting mat
There is no need to spend a lot of money on a custom cutting mat – a longish off-cut from a piece of mount board is ideal.

MATERIALS:

You will need each of the consumable items that follow to make a basic frame. You can buy everything from a specialist supplier (see Resources for details) or from a mix of online and your local hardware store or timber merchant. If you're planning to make more than a few frames, it's worth buying several pieces of mount board at once to justify the delivery cost. Alternatively, see if your local frame shop will sell you a sheet or half of one. Don't worry, they won't feel competition from you as a hobby framer and may even be happy to offer advice.

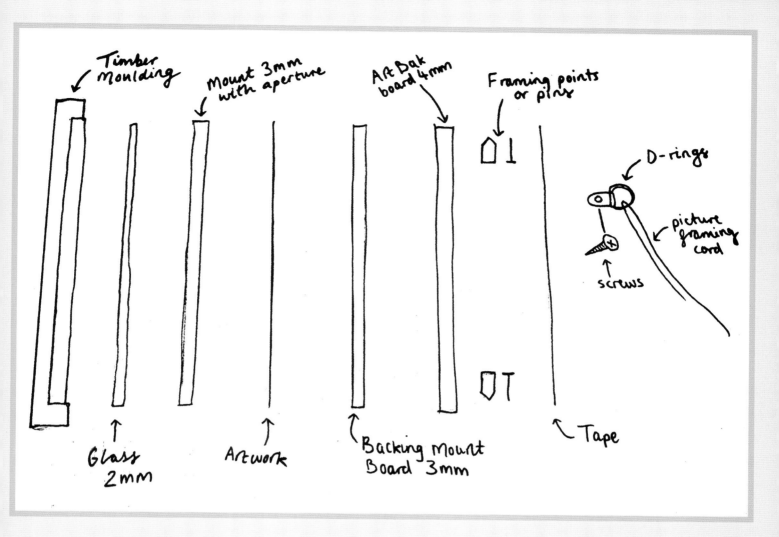

ANATOMY OF A BASIC FRAME

Moulding The timber surround, whether shaped or flat.

Rebate An overhanging lip inside the timber moulding that holds all the internal elements of a frame in place – glass, mount, picture, backing board, Art Bak board.

Glass Protects the picture from dust and dirt.

Mount This separates the image from the glass. It is usually made of thick cardboard – known as mount board. The artwork is attached to the back of the mount with two small pieces of tape at the top.

Aperture The cut-out 'window' in the mount through which the artwork is visible.

Backing board A second mount with no aperture to support the back of the picture.

Art Bak A fluted cardboard that gives rigidity and protection to the frame. Fixed with small nails or framing tabs, and brown self-adhesive framing tape (to stop dust).

Fixings Items that secure the frame in some way, such as screws, nails and D-rings.

Job lot of mouldings.

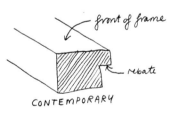

CONTEMPORARY

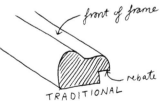

TRADITIONAL

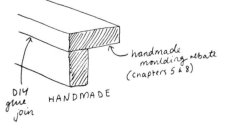

HANDMADE

Mount board

Generally supplied in A1 sheets, or available cut into smaller sizes from your local frame shop if you do not wish to buy in bulk. Available in many colours, this thick cardboard usually has a white core that looks smart when cut at an angle with a mount cutter. The projects in this book can all be completed using basic white mount board. If possible, choose an 'acid-free' variety which will prevent artwork from yellowing over time.

Art Bak Board

Fixed to the rear of the frame, and held in place with panel pins or framing tabs, this was traditionally made from hardboard or MDF. The modern alternative is fluted cardboard, such as Art Bak, which can be cut with a Stanley knife and comes in an acid-free variety to protect your artwork over time.

Brown self-adhesive framing tape

Used on the back of the frame to prevent dust sneaking into the frame, this is a paper-based self-adhesive tape on a roll.

Wood glue

A strong wood glue such as Everbuild All Purpose Weatherproof Wood Adhesive is your ally. Stronger than normal PVA glue (and stronger in fact than the wood itself), it also dries fast (touch dry in ten minutes in the case of Everbuild).

Timber mouldings or flat timber

It is perfectly possible to complete all the frames in this book without using specialised picture frame mouldings. These account for much of the high cost of commercial picture framing. If you buy flat timber and/or decorative bevels from your local hardware store or builder's merchant, bond them together with wood glue and paint them yourself, you will save money (see Chapter 5 and Chapter 8 for how to do this).

Alternatively, look on sites such as eBay and Gumtree for 'job lots' of framing mouldings from shops closing down or refreshing their end of lines.

I'm an inveterate bargain hunter and my best ever buy was a kilometre of mixed picture framing mouldings for £28. This 1,000 metres of timber saved me several thousand pounds (a small sample is pictured here, by our basketball hoop). If it's pre-stained or pre-painted in colours you don't like, simply apply a coat of primer before following my paint effect suggestions.

Panel pins

These are small ¾in pins used to keep each corner of a frame secure. They can also be used to hold the Art Bak board in position during assembly.

Fixings

You'll need some form of fixing to hang your frame. Two metal D-rings and picture cord are suitable for most, but a sturdier frame – or a memory box – will require heavier-duty fixings, such as two metal 'hanging strap' fixings.

Paint

So little paint is used in picture framing that you can use up all sorts of leftovers from previous craft or DIY projects. You'll need only a few tablespoons of paint, if that, for an average frame.

As long as all elements mixed together are water-based, you can tint basic white matt emulsion with coloured emulsion, acrylic paint or paint pigments.

Other paint options include tiny pots of enamel paint or gloss paint. You can also use spray paint before assembling your frame for a modern look, or wash your frame with watercolour paint followed by a coat of satin varnish or Danish oil for a soft, aged (waterproof) appearance.

Water-based Varnish

Polyvine's decorator's varnish (matt, satin or gloss finish) can be tinted with pigment or metal powder to make a glaze you can apply with a small artist's brush to your frames (see Chapter 5: Box Frames).

Search for 'nail art suppliers' online to buy small quantities of gold, copper or silver metal powder.

Picture-framing cord

Household string is acceptable, but for a strong non-stretch solution it's worth investing in a roll of picture-framing cord.

Acid-free tape

This cream or white tape is used to hold the top of an image to the back of the mount. If not acid free, you risk the tape discolouring over time. For a more basic option,

INSIDER TIP:

If you are going to make more than a handful of frames, consider investing in a Hand Operated Tab Driver instead of using panel pins and a hammer to secure the Art Bak board. This clever hand tool has a magazine loaded with a strip of pointed tabs. Each time you press the trigger, a metal tab is fired into the frame to secure the board before taping – which speeds up your frame assembly. Choosing flexible points for the gun enables pictures to be removed with ease.

Alternatively, as a halfway house, you can buy a box of Push Points from a framing supplies company; these angled points can be pushed into the sides of a frame with the tip of a flat-head screwdriver.

BUYING GLASS

In a word (two words actually): Buy glass. This is especially true when learning to picture frame or if you plan only to frame a few pictures a year. Glass is cheap. I've tried investing in big sheets and cutting them down and there is wastage, failure and too many broken shards where it all went wrong. Find a good trade supplier – such as Shaw's Glass in the South East – and place an order for '2mm float glass'.

It is always better to order the glass after your frame is finished as this enables you to measure the rebate (the place in the moulding where the glass sits). Home-made frames are rarely truly square (mine aren't anyway, so well done indeed if yours are). Measure the rebate and reduce by 2mm to ensure that the glass you have ordered will fit.

The only exception to the above is when you plan to up-cycle old frame glass. I have a friend who loves to trawl car boot sales for artworks and she often passes on unwanted frames allowing me to plunder the glass for my own projects.

If money is an issue you can definitely save some by searching for large pictures in charity shops. If they cost less than £5 they might be worth buying. An Amazon-bought glass cutter with a white-spirit filled reservoir paid for itself with the first large piece of charity-shop-salvaged glass I successfully trimmed to size.

use decorator's masking tape (avoid using Sellotape as it yellows and dries out fairly quickly).

Glass

Unless you are framing an oil or acrylic, you will require a piece of glass (or sheet of Perspex) as a transparent protective surface to keep your image and mount clean and dust-free.

This is especially true for the delicate surface of watercolours or drawings in pencil, pen and ink, charcoal or pastel. It's also a good idea to use a sheet of glass or Perspex if you are framing a printed image with a cardboard mount – the paper surface is vulnerable to damage and over time will accumulate dust.

Some paintings don't require glass, such as acrylics and oils that are sealed with varnish. Glass can also obscure fine brush strokes and surface detail – an important factor in many paintings of this type.

OPTIONAL MATERIALS:

Primer – a base-coat paint with a 'key' (i.e. a slightly rough surface) that enables you to apply a new finish over the top without the hassle of removing the existing paint. This is particularly important if you are putting a water-based paint (i.e. emulsion) over an oil finish (most factory mouldings).

NB: *A couple of projects require specialist materials – such as cork tiles, copper sheet, and gold leaf – these are detailed in the 'ingredients' section of the relevant chapters and in the Resources section at the end of the book.*

INSIDER TIP:
Pigment is the pure colour used to make paint or ink. By mixing pigments with a binder (such as emulsion or decorator's varnish) you can create your own paint or coloured varnish in any shade you require, and in tiny quantities. It's a good value method of acquiring limitless custom colours for your frames. I use Polyvine Universal Acrylic Colourant in 50g pots. The following shades enable you to mix most colours you will need for framing, by using a few drops and stirring into a few tablespoons of emulsion, before tweaking if necessary: Yellow Oxide (a dirty yellow); Raw Sienna (a light brown); Teak (a dark brown); Ultramarine (blue); and Red.

CHAPTER ONE

HOW TO MAKE A BASIC FRAME

ONE OF THE most enjoyable aspects of framing is choosing the colour of the frame by looking at the image and deciding which tone to highlight, or contrast. Here I have chosen a contrasting blood-red emulsion paint – informed by the pen artist's stamped red signature – and sealed this with a delicate glaze of gold dust to add sparkle.

The principle of making a frame remains the same whether it is large or small, rectangular or square: four lengths of wood are connected at four corners.

For a square frame, the lengths of wood are all the same length.

These Chinese-inspired frames look pretty striking, but are easy to make.

The colours of both the wooden moulding and the mount have a big influence on the way you see the colours in the picture you are framing.

If one colour is dominant in your print or painting, it's usually a mistake to choose a frame or mount of the same colour. But matching the colour of mount or frame to one or two less dominant colours in the image can make these visually 'pop' in an appealing or striking way, and entirely changes the experience of the image.

Envisage a photograph of a sunset: a pale pink or orange mount will tell one story. However, if the image features a tiny blue house in the foreground, using this shade in the frame or mount will accentuate and draw the eye there first.

You can also use tonal contrasts in the frame. A very delicate pastel watercolour can look striking in a black or dark frame. Meanwhile, the rich colours of a dark painting can be heightened, or left to speak for themselves, when surrounded by a white or pale moulding.

The great thing about making your own frames is that decisions are affordably reversible. If you don't like the look just change the colour of the mount, or repaint the frame. This costs peanuts.

For a rectangle, two of the pieces of wood are longer (or shorter) than the other two.

The wood used for picture framing is known as a moulding, and in most cases it has a rebate cut in it for the glass and image to sit inside. In Chapter 5, I'll show you how to make your own cost-effective mouldings.

When framing a picture, it's easier to cut the mount before making the frame – this way, you can be sure the frame fits precisely. So this is where we will start.

HOW TO MEASURE AND CUT A MOUNT

Whether you're showcasing a favourite piece of children's artwork or planning to display a treasured family heirloom, knowing how to cut a neat aperture in mount board will immediately give your project a crisp professional finish.

But although it looks the business, creating that appealing bevelled edge on the mount within a picture frame is actually very easy to achieve at home.

All it takes is one simple hand tool – a mount board cutter. These are readily available online for less than the price of a couple of mounts cut in-store for you. I've had mine for two decades and I've cut dozens of boards in that time with nothing more complex than the odd blade change – which involves unscrewing the unit and popping in a new blade.

The mount board cutter is sometimes sold together with a long straight-edge made of metal. This has a notch running its length into which a lug on the cutter is located, enabling the cutter to slide up and down in a perfectly straight line.

If you firmly press down on the straight-edge, as you slide the cutter across the mount board, wonky cuts are generally eliminated – although this can take a bit of practice. It's a good idea to make some test cuts on a spare piece of mount board to get the hang of it before making your cuts for real on your carefully measured board.

Equipment
- Mount board cutter and straight-edge
- Pencil
- Set square ruler
- Stanley or artist's scalpel knife

Ingredients
- Two pieces of mount board: the visible piece and a backing board of the same size which can be an offcut in any colour. Mount boards are generally sold in very large A1 sheets, but your local picture framing shop may be prepared to sell you offcuts if you want a smaller amount.

- A piece of scrap card or mount board no smaller than your finished project into which the blade of your mount cutter will sink. You could use a self-healing mat if funds allow, but buy one big enough to cope with the largest window you are likely to cut. Be warned: Stopping a cut midway is a recipe for a wobbly and unprofessional finish.

Method:
1. Flip the mount board and place it face down on a clean piece of scrap card. Measure the painting you want to frame and reduce both the vertical and horizontal measurements by 1cm to allow an overlap. For example, 40cm x 21cm – this measurement will be the size of your aperture.

2. To find the outside measurement of the mount, add a margin to the size of your window. For example, 6cm all round.

3. Jot down the figures on the back of the mount board, in this case 40cm + 12cm for the length, and 21cm + 12cm for the width.

NB: *Always remember to double the margin as there are two sides. Remember to add 6mm–8mm to the depth of the bottom margin as this visually grounds the image and is pleasing to the eye.*

4. Measure and mark up the finished mount size – in this instance a total of 52cm x 33cm – using a pencil and a set square ruler to ensure you have perfect right angles. (When the horizontal edge of the set square ruler rests against the horizontal edge of the mount

board this guarantees that the vertical edge of the set square will be at precisely 90 degrees, ensuring that your mount will be perfectly vertical as well.)

5. Make sure you are resting on your cutting mat or mount board offcut, and cut firmly along all the pencil lines using a Stanley knife by pulling the blade towards you. You may need to go over the line several times to ensure you cut all the way through.

6. Flip the mount to the reverse side and draw the measurements for your aperture on the rear by measuring in from the outside edge

of your mount and marking it – in this case 6cm at the sides and top, and 6.8cm at the bottom – in a couple of places. Join up the marks to make the aperture-to-be-cut, ensuring that the lines cross over and extend all the way to the edges of the mount; this will make it easy to locate the lines when the mount cutter and straight-edge are sitting on top of them.

7. Line up the straight edge with the pencil mark on the left-hand edge of the window and prepare to make the first incision with the mount cutter.

As well as ensuring you are cutting the left-hand edge first, always double-check you are cutting on the reverse side of the mount to ensure the bevel will be visible from the front. As a general rule of thumb, it's a good idea to start your cut a good three or four millimetres beneath each corner of the pencilled-in aperture. This ensures the corners are neatly cut out. You won't notice the extra few millimetres of cross-over in the finished work. Keep up a firm, slow and sustained pressure as you slide the mount cutter forward along the straight-edge to ensure the mount is cut all the way through.

NB: *Some mount cutters have an adjustable lug which enables the blade to be set more deeply if using thicker mount board. I tend to set it at the maximum to ensure a clean cut, following plenty of trial and error where one side failed to cut deep enough, ruining the entire window. I would like to save you from this time-wasting frustration.*

8. After the first left-hand cut, turn the mount 90 degrees clockwise to place the next line-to-be-cut on your left-hand side. Continue turning the board for the other two sides so you are always cutting on the left to ensure visibility of the bevel on the front of the mount. This might sound complex but will make sense when you do it.

9. Cut another piece of mount board as a backing using the same external dimensions as the first mount, but don't cut an aperture in this piece.

10. Take your painting and place it on the backing board and, with the right side facing forward, lay the mount containing the window aperture on the top. This should create a framing 'sandwich' where the image is held between the two pieces of mount board.

11. Gently move the image around until the placement is correct and then hold firmly and turn the 'sandwich' upside down. Gently lift off the backing board and weight down the artwork, so it stays in place within the window underneath.

12. Cut two 4cm pieces of acid-free tape or masking tape. Use them to attach the back of the painting to the top of the window mount, overlapping 2cm of the tape onto the painting or photograph you are framing.

Fix short pieces of tape across the two lengths of 2cm tape to secure them to the mount – so they look at bit like cartoon plasters.

Hanging the artwork or photograph from only two hinged points in this manner, enables the image to expand and contract when in the frame. It also prevents it from wrinkling, which is a real risk, so don't be tempted to add additional fixing points to the bottom

of an artwork or photograph. Our homes experience constant changes in humidity due to seasonal variation and cooking, and framed artwork and photographs are sensitive to this – they need to be free to move within the frame.

13. Flip the window with the painting attached to it the right way up and lay it down on the second piece of mount board ready to be inserted into your finished frame. Then cut a piece of Art Bak board to the same dimensions as your two mount boards.

MAKING THE FRAME

Now you have a completed mount, you are able to make a frame to fit its dimensions.

Equipment
- Mitre saw
- Ruler
- Pencil
- Mitre clamp
- Hand drill
- Hammer
- Punch
- Paint brush
- Sandpaper block

Ingredients
- Sufficient timber to make a four-sided frame, plus 20 per cent for wastage
- Wood adhesive

- Wood filler – or make your own using the Insider Tip on Page 38
- Paint in your chosen colour
- Glass to fit
- Two pieces of mount board larger than your image and cut to size, one with an aperture.
- A piece of Art Bak board cut to the same size as your mount
- 20–30 ¾in panel pins
- Brown self-adhesive framing tape
- Two D-rings and suitable short screws
- Picture-framing cord (or string)

Method:
1. Lift the mitre saw blade, and slide in a length of timber ensuring that the rebated side is facing you (the side that is flat should be pressed up against the back edge of the mitre saw). Secure the timber using the clamp on the saw, and cut a 45-degree angle on one end towards you (an inward cut).

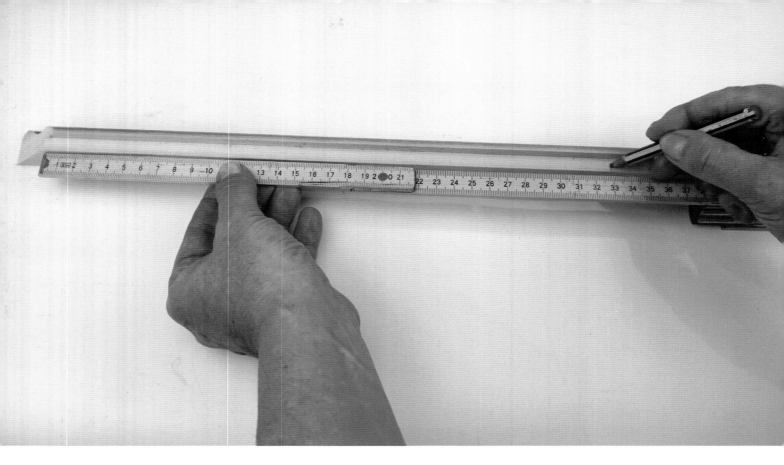

2. Use the ruler to measure from the inside corner just cut, and mark on the rebate the required length for the second cut – you want this to be the length of one side of the mount plus 2mm, to allow for a bit of wiggle room when you fit the mount.

3. Replace the moulding into the mitre saw, again with the rebate facing you. Now rotate the saw to the opposite 45-degree position in preparation for an opposing diagonal inward cut. Move the timber into position carefully so that the pencil mark you have made corresponds precisely with the cut of the saw.

You will now have a piece of timber with opposing angles at either end.

4. Prepare to make another identical cut piece in the remaining timber. First, you will need to rotate the mitre saw back to the original 45-degree angle and cut off a few inches of excess wood. You have now cut the first angle on the second piece of timber.

5. You now need to mark the position of the second cut, to ensure both pieces will be the same length. Do so by removing the moulding from the mitre saw. Rest the first cut piece of timber on top of this long piece – taking care to ensure that the bottom surfaces are touching and the first cut corners are matched up. Mark with a pencil.

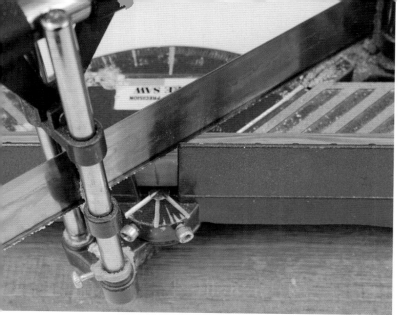
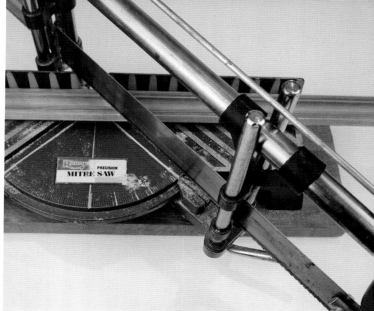

6. Line up the pencil line under the blade so it will cut the right length – too long or too short is a problem, and you'll have to start again with the second piece.

7. Make the second opposing cut in the second piece of timber. You should now have two pieces of the same length.

8. Repeat the process for the third and fourth pieces of timber, remembering to measure the other dimension of the mount board and to add 2mm of wiggle room to this length. Lightly sand both ends of all four pieces so they are smooth and ready to attach.

9. To assemble the frame from your cut pieces, take a long and a short piece of timber (or two equal pieces if the frame is absolutely square) and place pieces in the corner clamp with the longer piece on the left-hand side. Adjust the pieces until they fit together neatly and tighten both sides of the clamp.

10. Slightly undo the clamp on the shorter piece, lift out the timber and apply a few dots of wood glue to the exposed cut edge.

11. Clamp together again for real, and then use a small drill to make pilot holes that will enable a couple of panel pins to pierce the right-hand moulding and secure it to the moulding on the left.

12. Gently hammer the panel pins until they are flush with the surface of the moulding.

13. Use a punch and hammer to tap the tops of the pins 1–2mm beneath the timber surface.

   Repeat the entire assembly process to make up the other half of the frame, remembering to keep the longer piece on the left-hand side of the clamp.

INSIDER TIP:
To make your own sandpaper block – to ensure flat sanding – wrap a small strip of sandpaper around a timber offcut.

INSIDER TIP:

To make your own wood filler, mix a few drops of glue with a few drops of sawdust harvested from beneath the mitre saw. Once dry, this can be sanded like shop-bought filler.

You will now have two similar L-shaped pieces and are ready to assemble the frame. Bring together two of the exposed corners, as before, and join with glue and pins.

You may need to support the far corner of the frame as you assemble it. Measure the height of the clamp and use books to create a platform which can support the opposing corner of the frame. Keeping the frame flat while you glue the moulding together is important, not least so that it hangs flush with the wall.

14. Fill pin holes with wood filler. This can shrink back as it dries, so leave the filler slightly proud of the surface and sand when dry (this can take an hour or so).

15. Paint the frame with your chosen base colour; in this case I've used a lipstick-red emulsion that was leftover from a previous frame. I finished this with a gold dust glaze. The sash brush gives a lovely streak-free finish. Before you assemble the frame, make sure that your paint treatment is complete as you won't be able to paint the frame once the glass is in position.

INSIDER TIP:

How to make an easy, 'go-to' paint finish using nothing other than emulsion paint and wire wool.

You can paint your frames in a solid coat of emulsion and buff with 0000 wire wool, or go one step further to make this versatile 'go-to' paint effect finish for your bare wood frame. ▶

▶ To produce a two-tone effect buffed to a lustrous sheen with wire wool, put two level tablespoonfuls of matt emulsion paint in an empty yoghurt pot (or similar).

• Add acrylic paint or pigment if you want to change the shade. Stir thoroughly and paint all over the front and sides of the frame.

• When thoroughly dry, buff the paint with an apricot-sized pad of 0000 wire wool until it develops a lustre.

• Use a dry paintbrush to brush off any particles of wire wool and paint dust.

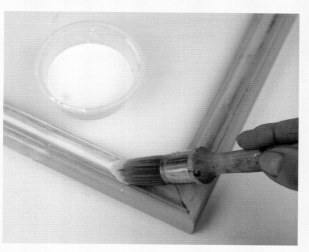

• To add a wash coat on top, put a level teaspoonful of emulsion of a different colour in another yoghurt pot (a cream or off white is good for the highlight coat). Add a tiny amount of brown paint to white emulsion to make up your own cream colour.

• Add a teaspoonful of water and stir until you have the consistency of single cream.

• Paint this very liquid paint over one side of the frame, ensuring the paint fills any surface details in the moulding.

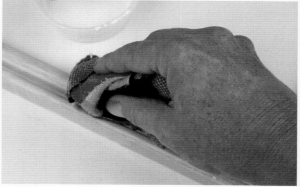

• Quickly wipe off the excess with an old rag (old socks are good for this), being careful to leave the wash coat where it has accumulated in any dips or indentations in ▶

the moulding – you are trying to highlight these by suggesting age.

• Repeat on all four sides of the frame.

• When thoroughly dry, buff the paintwork once again with the wire wool to create lustre.

• Use a dry paintbrush to brush off any particles of paint or wire wool.

This sample shows the effect of painting a blue wash coat on a white undercoat, and also a white wash coat on a blue undercoat.

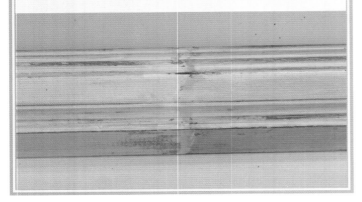

16. To order or cut a piece of 2mm float glass, first measure the inside of the rebate to ensure you have the correct dimensions. As handmade frames are rarely entirely square, it is advisable to measure the width of each dimension at both ends of the frame.

For example, perhaps one measurement is 29.8cm and the other is 30.2cm. In this case, you should use the smaller measurement and order glass in that size (i.e. 29.8cm). Unless you are massively out, the glass will still fit within the rebate. If things have gone a little haywire, and the frame is pretty asymmetric, it's best to take it to a glass shop where they can cut a piece of glass to your precise dimensions. Mumble something about the perils of a handmade product, if that makes you feel better.

Once you have a piece of glass appropriately cut to size – either by buying it made to measure or by cutting it yourself (see next page) – clean and insert it into the frame. Take care to ensure it remains as clean and dust-free as possible.

INSIDER TIP:
For added lustre, finish a painted frame with a DIY glaze of gold or copper dust. Add half a teaspoonful of metal craft dust (or glitter) to a dessertspoonful of varnish such as Polyvine's water-based decorator's varnish (or a sealer such as Mod Podge). Stir until mixed, then paint over the frame with a sash brush wiping off any excess with an old rag (or sock).

CUTTING GLASS

If you are bravely going to cut your own glass, ensure you have a flat surface. Line up the mount board you have already cut to size so that the left-hand side is flush with the left-hand edge of the glass.

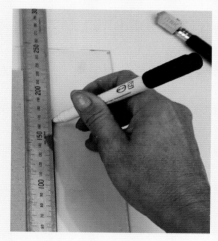 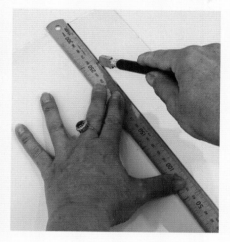 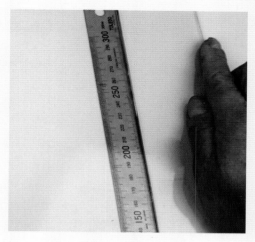

• Using a ruler for precision, mark a line with a dry marker pen (or felt-tip) for the excess.

NB: Wrap unwanted shards of glass in an old newspaper and seal with tape to prevent injury to those handling your rubbish. Better still, take them to a recycling centre to dispose of them safely.

• Slide the ruler under the glass to the left of the score line. Tap several times along the scored line with the end of the glass-cutter to cure it.

Place fingertips either side of the ruler and press down firmly. If it was a good cut the glass will break easily (the ruler acts as a pivot to snap the glass). For narrower pieces, break off the scored glass with pliers – which also works if not all the glass has broken over the ruler.

• Pressing down on the ruler or straight-edge firmly with your left hand, take the glass-cutter between your first and second finger in a pencil grip style, and gently draw it slowly and firmly towards you to score the glass. The glass-cutter scores the glass rather than cutting it and you should hear a 'ripping' sound if you are applying sufficient pressure. Keep the handle at a 90-degree angle to the glass and always score edge to edge. Never score in the same place twice, to prevent damaging the cutting wheel.

INSIDER TIP: Glass in frames needs to be clean and dust-free without any stray particles from a cleaning cloth. The most effective way to clean glass is using scrunched up sheets of newspaper and glass cleaner (or white vinegar in 50:50 dilution with water). Make a few squirts on one side of the glass and scrub firmly with the ball of newspaper, remembering to go right up to the edges. Hold flat against the light to check for any smears. Flip over and repeat. Handle with care to prevent fingermarks on the freshly cleaned surface. As you assemble the frame and add the mount and image, treble check for stray hairs or dust trapped beneath the glass. These can be removed with a paintbrush. Then check again before you seal everything up.

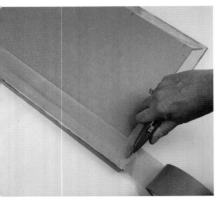

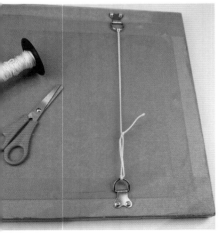

17. When assembling the picture, stand the mount, backing board and Art Bak board upright. This helps any dust or bits to fall out as you sandwich them together. Lay the frame face down again.

Carefully place the sandwiched boards into the frame and check again for dust by turning the frame over carefully. When you are confident the frame is dust-free, tap in panel pins with the hammer to secure the Art Bak board in position, paying particular attention to the corners.

18. Tape all four sides to keep out dust, using a Stanley knife to cut the tape near the edges. Smooth down the tape all around.

19. To hang your frame, add two D-rings through which you can thread the picture frame cord that will hold your picture. These should be screwed into the sides on the reverse of the frame, about one-third to one-quarter of the way down.

Mark their position in pencil, make small pilot holes with the hand drill, and fix screws in position with the screwdriver. Ensure the screws are short enough to not protrude through the front of the frame.

20. Cut a piece of picture framing cord, or household string if you prefer, 2.5 times the width of the frame. Fold in half and feed the loop end through one of the D-rings. Push the ends of the string through the loop and pull taut, before threading the string through the second D-ring and tying an overhand knot tensioned with another knot a third of a way along the cord. This reversible technique enables you to easily adjust the height that the frame hangs on the wall (if hanging pictures side by side, for example).

HOW TO ENHANCE AN ARTWORK USING DOUBLE MOUNTS AND FLOATING MOUNTS.

A mount is simply a window cut from a piece of card and placed over your drawing or painting. It is a vital element in the presentation of your picture, and protects your work from contact with the glass (important with a pastel painting, for example, where smudging against the glass would be possible). It also acts as a visual 'breathing space' to enable your artwork to be appreciated to the full.

A double mount adds a special extra touch – drawing additional attention to the image. It is nothing more complex than a sandwich of two mounts where the top aperture 'window' is larger than the bottom window – leaving a line of coloured mount around the

picture. This is a practical technique to use when framing an image that is thicker than a standard piece of art paper, such as this oil landscape on board by Ann Witheridge which I was given by her sister and a friend for my birthday.

The board on which Ann has painted her woodland scene is 4mm thick and I didn't want to hide this fact behind a standard aperture in a mount. Because of the thickness of the painted board, I also needed to 'float' the top mount to compensate – i.e. pack it out with small self-adhesive foam pads to ensure that while the top mount touches the glass in the usual way, the painting is still slightly recessed.

Float mounts also create an appealing shadow which further accentuates a treasured image or artwork.

I made the frame in the usual way, having salvaged and cut down this beautiful hardwood moulding from a large frame I've had for years, before enhancing the painting with a double mount. Read on for how to achieve this elegant look.

ARQADIA 8030

1. Place your painting on the back of a piece of mount board and mark out a generous margin on all four sides. In this case, 6cm plus an extra 6mm on the bottom edge, as explained in the mount section above. Measure in 4cm all around (4.6cm at the bottom) and use your set square and ruler (or straight edge) to draw intersecting lines on all sides.

2. Use this as a template to make a similarly sized second mount. This will go beneath the image after you cut the aperture. But first, measure off this second piece to make up a frame with timber moulding of your choice – following a method such as the Basic

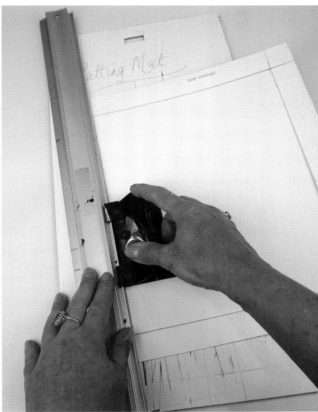

Frame outlined in Chapter 1 or the Box Frame Method used in Chapter 5.

3. Cut out the top mount using the bevel-edge cutter, as described on page 28-32.

If your artwork or image is on paper, you can now assemble the glass, double mounts, backing board and Art Bak in the way outlined on page 42.

If however you are planning to display an image which is thicker, such as this one painted on a 4mm board, you will need to 'float' the top mount.

HOW TO FLOAT MOUNT YOUR IMAGE

If you have a thick painting or image to frame, or if you just like the look of a shadow accentuating your treasure, you can 'float' the top mount in a way that creates a gap between the image and the glass.

To do this, stick twelve or so self-adhesive double-sided craft or decoupage pads to the underside of the top mount. These come in

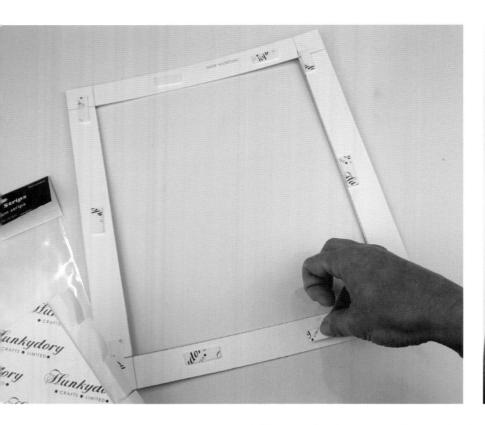

different thicknesses. 2mm thick pads are a versatile choice – you can use them as they are, or double them up (peeling off the backing paper between each layer) to achieve 4mm or even a high-rise 6mm, depending on the look you are after.

However, remember to check the depth of your rebate to ensure you will still be able to assemble the frame and secure the backing board and Art Bak with your chosen added thickness. You will tend to have more tolerance for this much deeper finish if you make a frame following the Box Frame Method in Chapter 5, which shows you how to create your own home-made moulding without the limitations of a generally narrow factory frame rebate.

After you have peeled off the paper on the self-adhesive pads, carefully place the top mount on the lower mount, ensuring the sides line up precisely. Press firmly to adhere the pads to the top mount.

Now that you have a neat mount board sandwich, it is time to fix your artwork to the centre of the lower mount before assembling the frame.

If you are framing a paper-based artwork in this way, four pieces of looped acid-free tape or masking tape (with the sticky side facing out) can be fixed on the rear near the corners of the artwork, and gently pressed into position.

For a heavier, three-dimensional artwork – such as my oil painting on board – use contact adhesive or household glue to secure the image if you don't mind it being permanent.

Then compress the artwork with a piece of spare mount board beneath a heavy object (such as your corner clamp) while it dries, before assembling the frame in the usual way outlined on page 42.

SUPERFAST 30-MINUTE FRAME FOR AN ACRYLIC OR OIL CANVAS

If you have an unframed canvas hanging in your home, now is the time to upgrade it with an easy and effective framing treatment. One bonus of oils or acrylics is that they don't need glass to keep them clean, or a mount to offer rigidity. This makes framing them much more straightforward.

Canvases are usually stretched over a sub-frame and stapled at the edges. You can hang them on the wall like this, but if you'd to add a smart yet simple frame follow these instructions.

NB: *This project has the added advantage that it doesn't require cutting a single diagonal mitre – all four saw cuts are straight not angled.*

• Buy a piece of planed flat timber from your local hardware store or timber merchant. This timber should be at least the same width as the depth of your canvas e.g. 2cm. (For a more dramatic 'box frame' effect make it somewhat wider. For example, if your canvas is 2cm deep, buy timber that is up to 5cm wide, as I have done here.) To buy the right length, measure both external dimensions of your canvas, multiply by two, and add 20 per cent.

• Use a mitre saw (or hand saw) set to 90 degrees and cut two pieces of timber that are exactly the same length as the sides of your frame (measure them individually and cut each to size if the sides are not absolutely square).

• Sand the ends and oil on all facets with Danish oil. Use a tinted oil or wood stain if you'd like to deepen the colour and bring out the grain. I've

This oil of Lake Como looks even more appealing with this simple frame.

used Osmo polyx Oil Tint 2073, a tinted oil with a satin finish (available from wood-finishes-direct.com, approx. £9 for 125ml, plus postage).

Alternatively, paint with two coats of black enamel paint or a coloured emulsion to accentuate a key colour in the painting.

• When the oil or stain is dry, place the canvas face down on your work surface and press the length of timber against it, ensuring it is flush with the painting at both ends. To secure, gently hammer in a few ¾in panel pins at equal distances down the length of the side (you may wish to use a bradawl or hand drill with a 2mm drill bit to make a pilot hole to ensure you don't split the wood). Spin the frame around and repeat on the other side, keeping canvas and timber flush against the work surface.

• Measure the width of the frame at top

and bottom, including the width of the attached timbers. Cut two more pieces of timber to this length and fit as before.

• Add D-rings and picture framing cord to the rear.

CHAPTER TWO
SIMPLE STRETCHED-CANVAS PANEL

THIS IS A SIMPLE but effective framing treatment, and really easy to do. It enables you to enjoy and savour a textile of any size or type as a work of art on your wall. You can use this technique to frame any kind of fabric – a favourite tea towel, a flag, a textile artwork or perhaps a section of an much-loved printed fabric (an old skirt for example) that you can no longer wear, but which can live on as an upcycled designer artwork.

The great thing about framing textiles is that it doesn't matter if they are not entirely square (or rectangular). Any untidy or ragged ends won't be seen because the fabric is stretched taut. You can also 'crop' or centre the piece as you wish.

In the past, I've framed fabrics including batique artwork and embroidered panels from my travels. But I found this rather lovely fabric painting among my mother Susan's possessions: I think she painted it in an art class in 2001. Rather than being tucked away in an envelope, we can now enjoy its autumn colours every day.

Living among trees in West Sussex, autumn is our favourite time of year and Bea has photographed this stretched-canvas frame against a standard hawthorn tree which we were given by a friend. Hawthorn is a tree with something for all seasons: thorny, architectural branches in winter; white blossom in spring; red berries in summer, followed by a vivid October palette – all rather reminiscent of my mother's fabric painting.

Equipment
- Mitre saw
- Pencil and ruler
- Mitre clamp
- Hammer
- Staple gun and staples

Ingredients
- Fabric panel

- Twelve panel pins at least 10mm longer than the width of the timber you choose. For example, when using 20mm timber, I use 30mm panel pins.

- Sufficient timber for the sub-frame. To calculate the quantity you need, add the lengths of all four sides of the fabric panel together, plus 40 per cent to allow for wastage and the all-important 'cross-brace' piece which will strengthen your work.

Generally speaking, the larger the frame the chunkier the timber needs to be to support it without bowing once the fabric is pulled taut.

In this case, my panel is approximately 240mm x 220mm and so I've used 20mm x 20mm timber which is more than strong enough. If framing a much larger or heavier textile, consider using timber that is 30mm x 30mm. You can make the frame even deeper if you wish, but from trial-and-error muck-ups, I don't recommend using timber that is any less than 20mm in any dimension.

- Additional timber if you wish to frame the sub-frame with an external frame, as I have done. Buy the same quantity of this timber. Although there will be no need for a cross-brace, it will be larger than the sub-frame you are going to encapsulate.

Because this external frame is not bearing the 'load' of the stretched timber and is for decoration only, the timber can be any size you wish but should be the same depth (or greater, if you like that look) as the original frame.

- Hooks and cord to display the work

Method:

1. Measure the canvas and make a note of the smallest dimensions. The idea is to try to avoid including unpainted/undecorated material on the front panel of the frame. It doesn't matter if some of the image is cropped over and laps on to the sides. In fact, this can look very striking, particularly if the image is large enough to allow it to flow over all edges and on to the back of the frame – in which case you won't need a secondary external frame.

FRAMELESS WONDERS

If your textile has a generous margin around it – as with this gentle screen-printed Buddha from Kathmandu – you can wrap the fabric around the sides of the internal frame, secure at the back with staples, and add D-rings to hang your work. There is no need for an external frame and you can forget steps 11 and 12.

2. To make the internal structural frame, use a normal hand saw (or your mitre saw set to a 90-degree angle on this angle) to cut five pieces of timber with flat ends. There is no need for mitre cuts when the corner joints will be hidden and you have a cross-brace for strength instead.

The top and bottom rail should be the same length as the horizontal measurement you took. To ascertain the length of the three vertical pieces which will slot into these, deduct the thickness of both the top and bottom rail from the vertical measurement or the frame will be too large.

3. Before you affix the internal frame, rest the pieces together and drape your fabric over them to check for mistakes – easy to make. When I first assembled this frame, I fixed the connecting pieces to the outside of the horizontal rails and the frame was too long. I

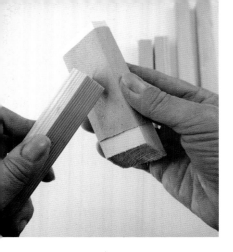
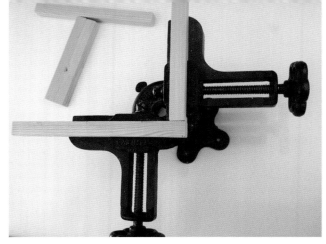

had to take it all apart and start again. So always check before you permanently fix your frame; removing panel pins from small pieces of carefully-cut timber is…annoying.

4. Before assembly, sand the cut ends of the timber battens for a neat finish that won't puncture your textile.

5. Use your corner clamp to glue and fix each corner by butting up the two flat surfaces against one another (rather than two 45-degree angled surfaces, as in the Basic Frame in Chapter 1).

6. After gluing, drill two shallow pilot holes in the end of the longer piece and tap in your panel pins so they pierce through to the shorter piece of timber.

7. Assemble the two opposing corners first, then join the other corners to form a rectangle. Glue in the central brace and secure with panel pins on both ends.

INSIDER TIP:
If your textile feels a little too delicate to be stretched and staple gunned, and you don't think it will cope with being placed under too much tension, carefully iron it before gently stretching it around a piece of Art Bak board cut to size. Use masking tape or brown self-adhesive framing tape to fix each side to the rear of the board. You can then mount it under the aperture in a standard mount, or 'float' mount it following the instructions on page 45-47.

8. Flip your textile so it is face down on a clean work surface or spare piece of mount board, and lay the frame on top.

9. Use your staple gun to attach the fabric to the frame. This will be either on to the sides or the back of the frame depending on your individual project. Work from the centre of the fabric and then outwards with the staples, to avoid creases. After doing both the ends, secure the textile to the top and bottom of the frame in the same way.

10. Leave the corners until last. Fold them in and secure with an additional staple. Don't be afraid to be quite firm with your fabric to ensure a crease-free stretch.

11. When finished, measure each side of the textile again (the thickness of the fabric and the staples will have changed the dimensions a little). You want the external frame to fit snugly around what you have actually made – give yourself permission cheerfully to sacrifice right angles on the altar of quirky in this instance.

Personally, I've certainly never worried too much about right angles – pleasing to the eye is generally the metric used in most Woodland Pie framing projects.

12. Assemble the external frame by clamping each corner as in step 5, one after the other, before applying wood glue and fixing with panel pins.

When the glue is dry – i.e. the frame is fully strong – gently push the sub-frame inside it. A good snug fit won't need any additional fixings, and not fixing it permanently in position has the added advantage that the textile can be more easily removed at a later date.

However, don't worry if you do end up with a bit of a gap, just use some brown self-adhesive framing tape on the rear to connect the two sub-frames together on all sides. If things are really dire and

you have quite a large gap, you can even tap on a bit of Art Bak or mount board to both frames with panel pins.

13. Affix D-rings to the back of the frame.

14. Add picture framing cord.

15. Your easy stretched-canvas panel is complete!

CHAPTER THREE

DECOUPAGE CORK, CHALK OR PEG BOARD FOR THE KITCHEN OR STUDY

THE ART OF DECOUPAGE – decorating an object using cut paper – has been around since at least the twelfth century and remains a versatile way to preserve paper keepsakes, such as favourite postcards, thank you letters or birthday cards. You can also use wrapping paper but choose the thicker variety as thin paper will wrinkle when glued.

When applied to a home-made frame, these recycled paper or cardboard images make a unique setting for a cork or chalk board, with an added dose of happy memories included. With a coat of varnish, they become durable and long lasting.

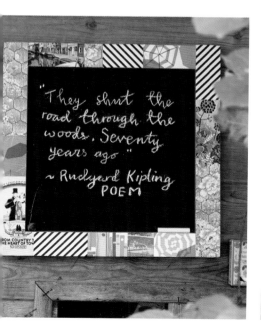

I tend to hang on to the prettiest thank you cards I receive for upcycling in this way, after I've displayed them with small wooden pegs on a cotton thread across my chimney-breast for a while. One friend often sends brilliantly Bohemian cards in colours I love, as does my cousin. Long live real cards.

Read on to find out how to give them an enduring life, rather than throwing them away – and remember that you can also decoupage such items as tea trays or even small pieces of furniture, following exactly the same simple method.

Equipment
- Sandpaper
- Corner clamp
- Paint brush
- Stanley knife
- Cutting mat (or mount board offcut)
- Hand drill or bradawl
- Hammer
- Punch
- Screwdriver
- Saw or hacksaw for the blackboard project

Ingredients
- Four strips of planed (sanded) timber, 6–8cm wide x 1–2cm thick
- A selection of cards or printed artwork
- Art Bak or mount board offcut
- Panel pins
- Wood glue
- Paint
- Brown self-adhesive framing tape
- Varnish (such as Polyvine water-based decorator's varnish)
- D-rings
- Picture-framing cord (or household string)

PLUS:
For the cork board:
- Piece of Art Bak board the size of your planned frame
- Self-adhesive cork tile
- Drawing pins or coloured map pins

For the blackboard:
- Piece of hardboard the size of the interior of your planned frame (the back of an old frame works well)
- Small tin of blackboard paint
- Chalk

For the peg board:
- Fabric offcut the size of the frame
- Thick cardboard or Art Bak board the size of the aperture in the frame
- Strong masking tape such as decorator's Frog Tape (or brown self-adhesive framing tape)
- One metre of ribbon or fabric trim at least 10mm wide
- Small wooden clothes pegs (or colourful paperclips)

Method:

1. First you need to calculate how much wood you need to buy. You can make a frame of this type any size, unless you are making the cork board version in which case you will need to work from the dimensions of your cork tile, multiply by four and add about 25 per cent for wastage.

For example, for a 30cm square cork tile you will need 30cm x 4 = 1.20m timber, plus 50 per cent wastage = 1.8m.

Use your mitre saw to cut opposing 45-degree angles in the timber. You need to produce four equally sized pieces, unless you have chosen to make a rectangular board in which case you will need two of one length, and two of another.

Remember that your cork tile (or chalk or peg board) will be fixed against the shorter interior side of the angled pieces – in this case 30cm. Whatever size your frame, remember that the interior measurement will always be shorter than the longer exterior measurement due to the extra material required to make the 45-degree cuts.

As this style of frame is made from flat timber, you will find it much quicker to make than a standard frame with a rebate. Using flat timber enables you to keep the mitre saw on the same angle throughout and flip the timber to cut the reverse side after you make each cut.

This should lead to less wastage than normal, but it's still a good idea to buy 50 per cent extra, just in case you go wrong and need to cut an extra piece.

Lightly sand the ends once all four angled pieces are cut. Before you do this, place them on top of each other to check they are virtually the same length – a 1–3mm difference is nothing to worry about. Anything more than this will require you to cut down the timber (if too long) or cut a fresh piece (if too short).

2. As with a normal frame, put two pieces into the corner clamp.

If you are making a rectangular frame ensure you clamp together two pieces of opposing length. If you attach the two long sides together by mistake you will be unable to assemble your Escher-like frame and will have to redo all your corners.

If your frame is square, as in my examples, it doesn't matter which pieces you glue together first.

Loosen one side of the clamp and remove the right-hand piece of timber. Squeeze a little wood glue onto the angle join and place back into the same position in the clamp. Drill two small 1-2mm pilot holes with your hand drill at the corner, and tap in panel pins to secure the corner. Use the punch and hammer to tap the tops slightly below the surface of the timber.

3. When you have two L-shaped pieces, join them together in the same way. This photo shows a support being used to stop the frame slumping in the back corner during assembly – all frames need to be flat. The decorative box I use to do this (which contains my supplies of ribbon and fabric tape) happens to be exactly the same height as the clamp base, but a stack of books works just as well.

4. It's rather satisfying at this point to see if the cork tile fits! If it doesn't, just use a Stanley knife and a metal ruler to trim it. If the aperture is slightly too large, don't worry, you will still be able to get a neat finish at the assembly stage. (If precision is important to you, you can always turn this frame into a peg or chalk board, and have another attempt at a more precisely fitting cork board frame.)

5. Look through your cards and work out a base paint colour for the sides of the frame that will complement the cards without overpowering them. This collection suggests a muddy turquoise.

The cards on the right (above) will get a lipstick red finish to bring out their vivid colour.

6. It's now time to paint your frame. You won't see much of the top painted surface, but painting the entire thing ensures that all edges will be fully covered.

   I don't use primer on bare wood for a project such as this, but I do enjoy using up leftover paint: This is a water-based eggshell garden

paint left over from painting the maypole at my children's primary school.

Acrylic paint will work well. So will poster paint or watercolour paint if sealed with decorator's varnish to make them waterproof. Alternatively, you could spray paint the frame gold or silver.

If making the blackboard frame, you might wish to paint the sides of the frame in blackboard paint too.

7. Using a Stanley knife, and cutting mat or mount board offcut, carefully trim the cards to the same width of the wooden battens that make up your frame. Make plenty of cardboard strips so you can select your favourites when you lay them out on the frame.

8. When you are happy with your composition, use a thin layer of wood adhesive to stick the cardboard onto your dry painted surface, wiping off any excess with a rag. If you don't have a glue spreader, sand down the end of a lolly stick or use a kitchen silicone spreader.

You can also use PVA glue, but I am impatient and like the quick-dry satisfaction of wood adhesive. It also provides a strong bond.

Trim off any excess cardboard when you lay out your card pieces: You'll achieve a more appealing finish if you butt them flush against one another, rather than overlapping, due to the thickness of the card.

9. Once the glue is dry, apply a layer of water-based decorator's varnish with a paintbrush. I'm using gloves because the varnish is pretty sticky.

Now you have a finished frame, it's now time to complete your individual project: cork board, blackboard or peg-board.

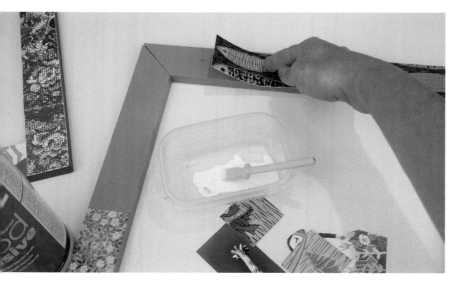

To finish the cork board:

10. To make a neat back for the frame, measure the internal dimensions and cut a piece of Art Bak board to a snug fit using your Stanley knife. Use a mount board offcut as a cutting mat if you don't have one.

Push the Art Bak into the frame, so it is flush with the back. Tape into position with brown self-adhesive framing tape on all four sides and press firmly from the front to ensure good adhesion.

11. Check again that the cork tile fits and trim to fit if necessary. Peel off the self-adhesive paper on the back of the cork tile, or apply a layer of glue if it's not the adhesive type. Push the tile down firmly into the frame so it sticks to the Art Bak. If the tile is slightly too small, position it in the middle of the aperture – the resulting shadow that appears around the cork tile will look entirely intentional!

BLACKBOARD PAINT

Blackboard paint is truly a blackboard in a can. I am awed by this product; it feels like a bit of magic, enabling any surface to be transformed in a couple of minutes into a chalkboard. With a can of blackboard paint in your possession, the old adage 'when all you have in the world is a hammer everything looks like a nail', comes to mind.

Why restrict yourself to a blackboard in a frame? Graduate to painting the back of your kitchen door or a nearby wall … I've painted two walls with blackboard paint, including the one next to my workshop loo. With chalk nearby, they soon fill up with aphorisms, and cheeky chat.

I've also used blackboard paint to create a greetings board in Bluebell, the shepherd's hut I rent out on Airbnb. To do this, just mask off an area of timber – a sanded plank or a chopping board work well – and paint two coats of blackboard paint in the marked-off area. Add D-rings to the rear, or drill holes to screw the board to the wall.

To finish the blackboard:

1. Place your completed frame on to a piece of hardboard – the back of an old picture works well for this. Alternatively, you could use a double thickness of Art Bak board and glue the two pieces together with wood glue for strength (weight them down while they dry if you do this, to prevent curling at the edges).

Push a corner of the hardboard into a corner of the frame aperture. Use a pencil to draw a line around the other two sides of the frame, marking out a square on the hardboard.

2. Cut the hardboard with a saw or hacksaw, following the pencil lines you have made. If you don't own a saw, you could also use a Stanley

knife by repeatedly marking an indentation along the pencil lines, before snapping the hardboard and tidying up the edges by paring with the Stanley knife. Double check the board fits snugly in the frame, and pare the edges further if required.

Paint with two coats of blackboard paint, leaving them to dry fully.

3. Lay the blackboard on your work surface and gently push the frame over the top until all surfaces are flush with the surface. Gently flip the frame over and apply tape to the back of the frame and the board, pushing gently from the front along the sides of the board to ensure good adhesion to the tape.

Your chalkboard is complete!

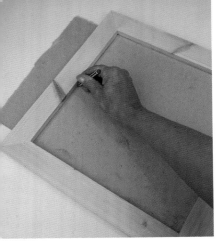

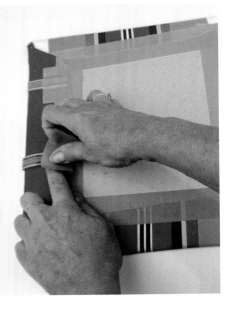

To finish the peg board:

1. As you did for the cork board, place your completed frame on to a piece of hardboard – again the back of an old picture works well for this. Alternatively, you could use a double thickness of Art Bak board and glue the two pieces together.

Push a corner of the hardboard into a corner of the frame aperture. Use a pencil to draw a line around the other two sides of the frame, marking out a square on the hardboard before cutting it with a saw, following the pencil lines you have made. If you don't own a saw, you could also use a Stanley knife by repeatedly marking an indentation along the pencil lines, before snapping the hardboard and tidying up the edges by paring with the Stanley knife.

2. Double-check that your hardboard mount fits the aperture in the frame, and if necessary carefully pare with the Stanley knife until it does. Then lay the board on your chosen fabric offcut. I've chosen a thick cotton 'deckchair' style fabric, but any material will do.

Cut the fabric to size leaving a generous 5–6cm margin all around and iron the fabric after you cut it, to avoid wrinkles in your finished work.

3 Starting at the top, pull the fabric taut and attach it to the board with the masking tape. I've used decorator's Frog Tape, which is particularly sticky, but brown self-adhesive framing tape will do. After you have fixed the top, pull the fabric tightly and attach tape to the bottom edge, ensuring there are no creases on the front of the work.

Twist the board 90 degrees and fit the first side (now the top). Pay special attention to the corners to avoid any wrinkles on the front of the board. Before you affix tape to the final side, check the front to ensure the fabric is smooth, and tweak a bit, if necessary.

4. It's now time to attach the ribbon or fabric trim that will support the pegs. I've used a vintage woven cotton trim that came from a haberdashery shop having a sale, but any ribbon or tape works well, as does twine. The key thing is to ensure that you fit your chosen material as tight as possible without warping the board – you don't want too much sag.

Cut either two or three lengths of tape, depending on the size of your frame (I've chosen to have two rows of pegs, so have cut two lengths). Add 8cm to each end (i.e. 16cm for each piece of ribbon or tape) to allow for the width of the frame. Ensure a good grip at both ends by taping the ribbon on to the existing masking tape.

5. Insert the finished peg board into the frame, it should be a nice snug fit now you have added the fabric to it.

6. Finish on the rear by using brown self-adhesive framing tape to affix it flush with the frame. Push down from the front at the edges to ensure good adhesion.

Your peg board is complete!

Adding the fixings to all three frame types:

A. Whichever variation you have made, you can now flip the finished frame over and attach D-rings to the rear of the frame using the drill (or a bradawl) to make small pilot holes. Use your screwdriver to fit the screws – ensuring they are short enough to not pierce the front of the frame.

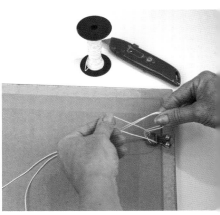

B. Cut a piece of picture framing cord (or household string) that is 2.5 times the width of the frame. Fold in half, and feed the loop end through one of the D-rings. Push the ends of the string through the loop and pull taut, before threading the string through the second D-ring and tying an overhand knot, tensioned with another knot a third of a way along the cord. This will allow you to easily adjust the height of the frame on the wall if required.

CHAPTER FOUR

GILDING A CHARITY SHOP FRAME

GILDING IS THE centuries-old craft of applying thin sheets of gold, silver or other metal leaf to make frames, furniture, or other decorative items appear to be made of precious metal.

Perhaps because of its history, it also gives the impression of being a specialised artisan skill; ornate gilding certainly requires expertise. But with a bit of practice, it is surprisingly easy to gild a couple of frames at home, using equipment and materials that will cost you less than £10 – as with these two charity shop mirrors which I've given a new lease of life with imitation gold leaf. You can apply real 23-carat gold leaf, but imitation leaf costs much less and creates a very realistic look.

I've often been asked to frame children's artwork, and for my son, Willem, this epic turtle homework definitely deserved special treatment. My daughter Bea completed the companion piece to spur him on, as he grappled with a fine liner one evening. Happy memories immortalised in an over the top frame treatment.

Anyway, read on to discover my 12-step guide to super-easy gilding.

Equipment
- Sandpaper
- Paint brush
To take frame apart:
- Stanley knife
- Pliers

To re-assemble frame:
- Hand drill
- Brown self-adhesive framing tape
- Fixings such as D-rings (if existing ones cannot be re-used)
- Picture framing cord
- Screwdriver

Ingredients

- An old frame
- Red paint

Gold leaf equipment (see resources) including:

- Fake gold leaf sheets
- Size (a special sticky glue for gold leafing)
- Soft brush or cotton wool
- Water-based Varnish

Optional: Art Bak board if existing frame back is not suitable for re-use

Method:

1. Find a suitable frame that fits the image you want to showcase, such as this lovely vintage hardwood glazed frame with less lovely pastel clowns.

Most charity shops have a few old frames for sale and if you take your measurements and a tape measure with you a rummage might produce the perfect candidate.

Check your chosen frame is large enough to include a mount around your artwork if you plan to include one.

If you can't find a frame of suitable size, you can of course make a bespoke frame instead, following the instructions in Chapter 1: Making a Basic Frame or Chapter 5: Box Frames for Photographs.

2. Take apart the old frame – this is fun because you never know what you'll find inside. Sometimes there is an artist's signature, or an invoice from the original framing company. It can also prove satisfying to one's inner nerd to see how the frame was constructed.

Use a Stanley knife to cut away the paper backing or tape and tear off as much paper as necessary to release the contents. Use pliers to remove the old pins holding the back board in place. You may need to be persuasive; try rocking them side to side. Prise out every pin, even if the backing board comes away after half are removed. It's safer that way.

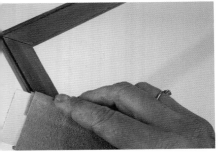

3. Gently coax out the contents of the frame. Keep the board (if still in re-usable condition) and clean the glass using glass cleaner or a 50:50 mix of vinegar and water, and scrunched up balls of newspaper. You may need to wash the glass on both sides with warm soapy water and a non-scratch scouring sponge first, if it is particularly dirty.

4. Sand the wooden frame back a bit to get rid of any flaky varnish or paint and to ensure a 'key' – a slightly roughened surface so that the size (gold leafing glue) will make a good bond with the surface.

5. Traditionally, gold leaf had an undercoat of 'boule' – a classic red paint that glows through the gold leaf and warms up its appearance. You can make up a DIY boule by using red emulsion, eggshell or acrylic paint. A water-based finish will obviously dry more quickly.

It's a good idea to place a few timber off-cuts on your work surface before you put the painted frame down to dry; this prevents the edges sticking to the table or protective newspaper and speeds up drying times.

6. When the frame is fully dry, lightly sand with fine sandpaper to create a smooth surface and remove any wrinkles in the paint.

Now you are ready to prepare the surface to receive the fake gold leaf. To do this, you need to apply 'size' – a special sticky glue with a long 'open' time, meaning it takes ages to dry and can be gilded for up to 24 hours after it is applied.

I bought this neat little hobby kit from eBay for my projects: it contains a small bottle of size – perfect for several projects – and a soft natural hair brush which is used to remove stray gold dust from the surface of the frame after application. You can also use cotton wool for this part.

INSIDER TIP:

Gold leaf and fake gold leaf is supplied as small sheets in packs where each leaf is separated by a dusted or waxed paper to prevent them from sticking together.

You may not be able to tell the difference between a good imitation and the real thing – but there is a huge difference in price.

Real gold leaf is 22 or 23-carat gold that has been hammered into thin sheets by gold beating. Being 100 per cent gold, albeit an extremely thin layer, it costs around £45 for twenty-five loose leaves measuring around 8cm x 8cm. It is also incredibly delicate and cannot be touched with bare hands – you have to pick it up with a soft brush.

A much more affordable option is imitation gold. This is either 'gold on base', where a microscopically thin layer of gold has been attached to a foil base; or fake gold leaf, which is made from an alloy (mix) of copper and aluminium. A pack of 100 x 7cm x 7cm sheets of fake/imitation gold leaf costs around £4. This will make you much more relaxed about applying it and happy to experiment.

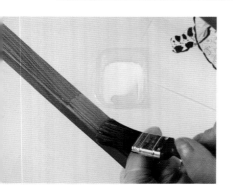

7. Use a standard paint brush to apply the size as smoothly as you can without streaks; a sash brush gives a streak-free finish. Leave the size to go tacky for about twenty minutes. Depending on the type of size you use, you'll have up to 24 hours to apply the gold leaf anyway.

8. If your frame is narrow, cut the gold leaf books in half with a Stanley knife to prevent wastage (make sure each half is left with part of the gummed protective paper at the top so you can open

them easily to press down the gold). Imitation gold leaf is easier to handle than real gold, but gloves will still stop it sticking to any moisture on your fingertips.

9. Work your way around the frame pressing the gold leaf on to the frame through the waxed paper. Overlapping the edges of the sheets a bit is a good idea to ensure full coverage; any excess can easily be dusted off later and won't leave a join because gold leaf is so thin – it feels more like applying a dry liquid than a sheet material.

10. When the entire frame is covered with leaf, use the soft brush (or a ball of cotton wool) to gently brush off any loose metal. It's best to use a natural fibre or gold leaf brush as the plastic fibres in a standard paint brush may scratch the gold finish.

INSIDER TIP:
To add a vintage look to your gold-leafed surface, rub a little paint thinner on a rag over the surface of your gold-leafed frame to reveal a little of the red boule paint underneath.

11. Fill in any obvious gaps with brushed off pieces of leaf, or with a small fresh piece. If you find areas where leaf will not stick, just re-size this area and repeat the process above.

To finish the frame, paint with water-based decorator's varnish (or spray-lacquer if you have some) to create a more durable surface, although this part is optional. Then make up your frame in the usual way – see Chapter 1 Fitting a Mount (page 28) for instructions on how to do this.

12. Use panel pins to hold a new piece of Art Bak cut to size, or salvaged back board, in position. Seal with brown self-adhesive framing tape.

Finally, add D-rings and picture framing cord.

Your gilded frame is complete!

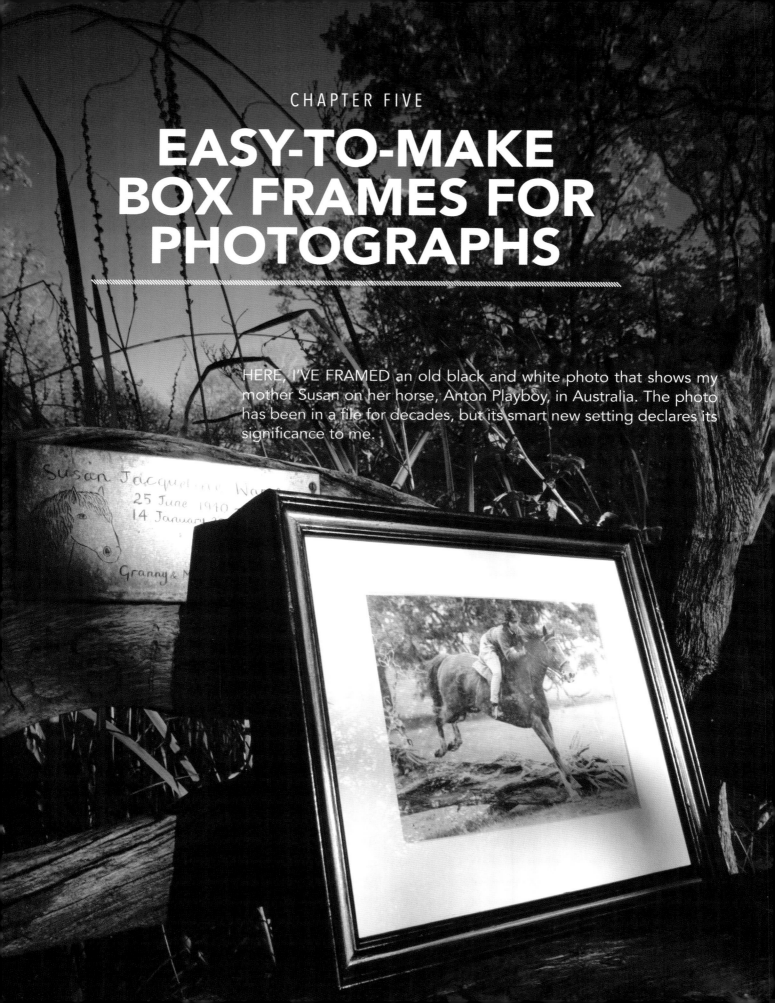

CHAPTER FIVE

EASY-TO-MAKE BOX FRAMES FOR PHOTOGRAPHS

HERE, I'VE FRAMED an old black and white photo that shows my mother Susan on her horse, Anton Playboy, in Australia. The photo has been in a file for decades, but its smart new setting declares its significance to me.

Box frames can be expensive to have custom-made in picture framing shops due to the cost of the deeper rebated timber they require. However, I've developed an approach that enables you to make up your own impressive box frames to almost any dimension – and all for the cost of joining two pieces of timber with wood glue.

The front piece of timber can either be shaped or flat. This is then glued to a length of flat planed timber that is deeper than it is narrow. Because the front timber is wider than the back piece, gluing them together automatically creates a rebate that keeps the glass and mount in place.

When the glue is dry, you can then use your mitre saw to cut your DIY box frame moulding into four pieces in the usual way. This really does save money.

Although black and white photographs are traditionally framed in black, there is nothing to stop you painting your frame any colour you wish.

For this photograph of an English rose, taken by a friend and given to me as a thank you card by her daughter, I made a small box frame before hand-tinting matt emulsion with a drop of cerise paint and a dab of yellow, to match the flower's delicate shade of pink.

When the paint was dry, I added a slender hand-painted line of silver gold dust in Mod Podge sealant along one facet to make it gleam in a manner suggestive of beaded dew on petals.

You can frame any image following the technique below; it doesn't have to be a photograph.

Equipment
- Wood glue
- Small clamps
- Picture frame corner clamp
- Ruler or tape measure
- Set square

- Stanley knife
- Mount cutter and straight-edge
- Pencil
- Mitre saw
- Sandpaper
- Wood filler (or wood glue with sawdust)
- Paintbrush
- Wire wool
- Hand drill with 1–2mm drill bit
- Screwdriver

Ingredients

- A photograph or other image

- Mount board

- A flat or shaped piece of timber, or a timber picture frame moulding, for the front face of the frame. Timber merchants and hardware stores often have a carousel of shaped and bevelled mouldings and beadings for around £4–6 for a length

- A piece of planed 'finished' timber the for the sides of the frame. To calculate the length see Method Step 1 (below).

- This piece should be slightly narrower than the timber used for the face of the frame – so that when the two pieces of timber are glued together, the all-important rebate is created, keeping the glass and picture mount in place.

- Wood glue

- Masking tape or acid-free tape

- Paint (emulsion or enamel, for example)

- Brown self-adhesive framing tape

- Panel pins

- D-rings and picture framing cord (or household string)

- Art Bak board

Method:

1. Place your image on the reverse of a piece of white mount board and mark up your chosen margin by adding 4–6cm around the edges, plus another 5–6mm to the bottom edge. A set square will make this quicker than taking repeated measurements with a ruler.

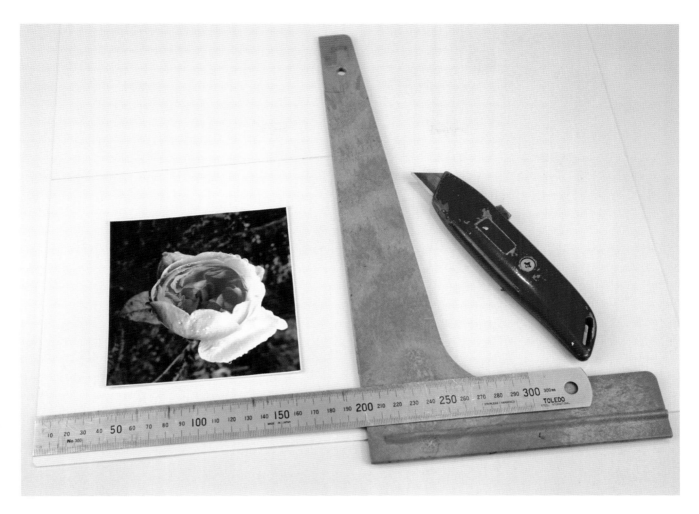

Cut the mount to size with a Stanley knife on your cutting board (or mount board offcut).

Use the mount to calculate the length of the two timber pieces you will need to buy. To do this, measure both external dimensions of your mount, add together, multiply by two, and add 50 per cent for wastage. For example, to frame a mount that measures 30cm x 20cm you will need to buy timber that measures 150cm (30 + 20 x 2 = 100 + 50 for wastage).

Buy both pieces of timber detailed in the ingredients list, to this dimension.

You can make the frame as deep as you like it, but 3–6cm looks effective, depending on the size of the mounted image.

2. Apply glue to the narrow side of the rear timber and bond it to the piece that will form the front of the frame, ensuring that one side is flush and leaving the other side as an overhanging lip, or 'rebate'.

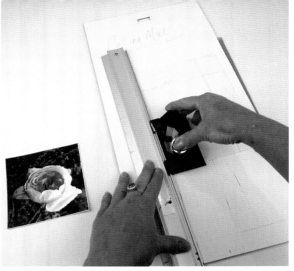

3. Bond with small clamps. If you don't have clamps, you can use strips of masking tape wound tightly around the bonded timber in five or six locations. When you add these, take care to ensure that one side of the lower timber remains flush with the outside edge of the top timber.

Use a few panel pins to hold the top timber in place as the glue dries, if necessary. Partially tap them in.

4. While the glue is drying thoroughly (refer to the instructions on the glue bottle), cut the aperture in the back of your mount, following the instructions in Chapter 1 page 28.

5. Lay the aperture in your mount over your picture, and position according to taste.

6. Holding the image carefully in position, tape the photograph to the rear of the mount using masking tape or acid-free tape in a classic 'plaster' configuration.

7. When the bonded timber has dried, place the back of the moulding you have made against the back of the mitre saw – ensuring that the rebate or overhang, is facing you. Clamp into position and saw the first 45-degree inward diagonal – as shown.

8. Place the inside of the timber against the long side of your mount and make a pencil mark, adding 2mm for a bit of wiggle room so it is easy to fit the mount when the frame is assembled.

If you are making a large frame, or your uncut timber is very long, you may need to use a tape measure for this stage if holding the timber against the mount is not practical.

Place the timber back into the mitre saw, on the right-hand side, and move the blade across in preparation for cutting the second 45-degree inward angle. Make sure that your two cuts are facing towards each other.

9. You will now have to rotate the saw back to the other 45-degree angle and cut off a few inches of excess wood. You have now cut the first angle on the second piece of timber.

When you have done this, mark the position of the second cut. Do so by resting the first cut piece of timber next to the long piece – taking care to ensure that both pieces of timber have the bonded piece uppermost and pointing outward. Mark with a pencil and cut the second angle. You should now have two pieces of the same length.

Measure the short side of the mount and repeat, giving you four cut pieces.

10. Sand all cut ends.

11. Assemble the first frame corner by taking the longer side in your left hand and the shorter side in your right hand. Insert them into the corner frame clamp so they make a perfect right angle. Apply glue to the right-hand piece and clamp into position.

Drill shallow pilot holes with a 1–2mm drill bit so that the panel pins won't split the timber. Tap them in with the hammer, and then use the hammer and punch to tap them one or two millimetres beneath the surface of the timber.

For more detail, see directions on page 36-38.

12. Make up the second L-shape frame piece. Then join both L-shaped pieces together to form a frame. In this photo, you can clearly see the rebate that has been made.

Fill the holes with filler or wood glue and sawdust. Sand smooth when dry with fine grade sandpaper.

When the glue on all four corners of the frame is dry, it's time to paint your box frame. For my mother's riding photo I used two coats of black enamel. A frame won't suffer significant wear and tear (unlike

a piece of furniture) so I don't bother using primer or base coat on new timber.

To frame the rose, I've hand-tinted some household emulsion to a delicate pale pink that complements the photograph.

When you paint the frame, it's a good idea to support it on a couple of timber offcuts to aid drying and prevent it sticking to newspaper, for example. When dry, add another coat.

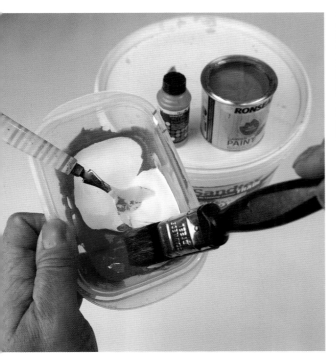

14. Rub down with wire wool after the second coat to create a natural polished lustre.

If you prefer to use a two-tone emulsion finish, follow the steps on page 39.

15. If you wish, enhance your frame with a hand-painted line of silver-coloured glaze. You can mix your own by adding metal powder (or real glitter) to Mod Podge, PVA glue or decorator's varnish.

16. When all paint is dry, assemble the frame by cleaning a piece of glass that has been cut to size, before adding the mount, backing board and Art Bak.

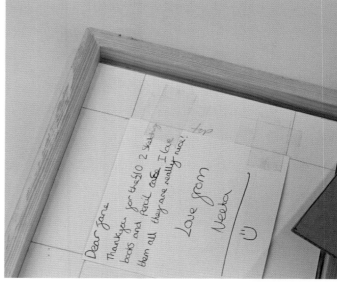

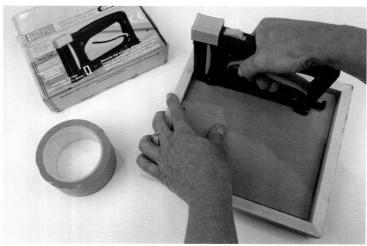

17. As this is a box frame, you are likely to have a generous gap behind the frame. Press down to ensure there are no gaps as you fit the Art Bak using small pins (see page 42 step 17) or by using a framing gun for speed and accuracy. Remember to check – at least once – there is no dust trapped under the glass before you do this.

18. Once the Art Bak is in position,

tape each side in turn with brown self-adhesive framing tape to keep dust out. Due to the depth of the frame, you will need to score both ends of the overlapped brown tape before taping on the next piece.

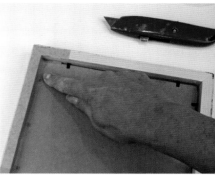

19. Carefully push the cut section of tape into the recess so it adheres to the side of the frame as well as to the Art Bak, for a neat finish.

20. Now add D-rings to the rear of the frame; marking with pencil, drilling small pilot holes with a 1–2mm drill bit, and adding small timber screws.

Finally, cut a piece of picture-framing cord (or household string) to length and tie it by following the instructions on page 42 step 20.

Your handmade budget-busting box frames are complete!

CHAPTER SIX

EMBOSSED COPPER HOLIDAY FRAME

THIS IS ONE of my favourite projects because the frame draws upon another craft to become a series of images itself. It's surely the Charlie Kaufman of framing projects.

The craft in question is metal embossing, which is hugely fun

to do and in this case involves working with copper – a lustrous, extremely soft metal. The process is satisfying and when finished the embossed images flicker in the light. It also requires minimal equipment.

I chose to make images of the tiny island of St Agnes, Isles of Scilly, where my family has been holidaying since the 1950s. For this reason I have called it a holiday frame, but the project works just as well with any set of embossed images be they abstract or more naturalistic, as you can see from these examples of a parrot and a bouquet embossed by my daughter Bea.

I've chosen to frame a photograph of Periglis – Britain's most south-westerly beach – and re-photographed it on the same wild beach in autumn, during a post-lockdown trip when I finished the frame. This was the first time I took a hot glue gun on holiday.

Making a holiday frame is a great way of immersing yourself in the present moment, as it encourages you to observe and draw your surroundings. It's also a DIY souvenir.

Equipment
- Mitre saw
- Mitre clamp
- Hammer
- Old household scissors – to cut copper
- Embossing tools – an old biro works just as well, as do sharpened lolly sticks, golf tees or small screwdrivers.
- Cardboard offcuts
- Pencil
- Hot glue gun (or strong household glue)

- Paint brush
- Hand drill (or bradawl)
- Screwdriver

Ingredients
- Two A4 soft copper sheets 0.1mm thick (See Resources on page 119)
- A holiday photo measuring approx. 18cm x 24cm if you wish to use a mount. Or at least 22cm x 29cm if you do not wish to use a mount
- Mount board if you wish to use it
- Art Bak board
- Two metres of planed (sanded) timber measuring 6–7cm wide. This ensures that a pack of two copper sheets will be sufficient (with some copper left over on which to practise embossing techniques). It also gives you a generous surface area for each image of around 6cm x 6cm or 7cm x 7cm.
- Paint for the sides of the frame – black enamel or copper/bronze paint depending on your taste.
- Pack of four mirror fixings and screws
- Masking tape or acid-free fixing tape
- Two D-rings to hang the frame
- Picture framing cord (or household string)
- Decorator's water-based varnish (optional)

Method:

1. To decorate a frame with square copper pieces, use your mitre saw to cut opposing 45-degree angles in the timber:

For a **rectangular** frame cut two strips of flat timber that at their longest are five times as long as they are wide (for the sides).

For example, if your timber is 7cm wide, your cut timbers should be 35cm long (7cm x five) on their longest side.

Then cut two pieces that at their longest are six times as long as they are wide (for the top and bottom). For example, if your timber is 7cm wide these will be 42cm long (7cm x six) on their longest side.

If you'd like to make a **square** frame, cut all four pieces of the same length – i.e. four pieces that are each five times as long (at their longest) as they are wide. In this example, these would all be 35cm long (7cm x five).

2. Lightly sand the ends once all four pieces are cut. Before you do this, place pieces of the same length on top of each other to check the length – a 1–3mm difference is nothing to worry about.

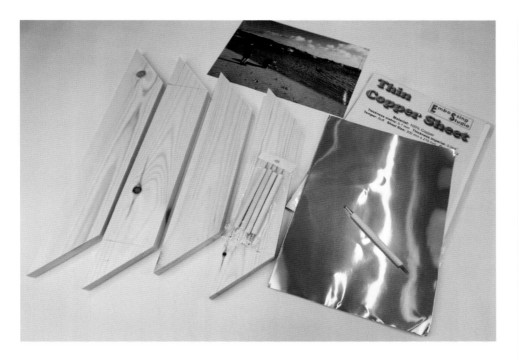

INSIDER TIP:
As this style of frame is made from flat timber with no rebate, you will find that it is quicker to make than a standard frame. Using flat timber enables you to keep the mitre saw on the same angle throughout and instead flip the timber to cut the reverse side after you make each cut – rather than reversing the saw blade angle as you would with a normal frame.

Anything more than this will require you to cut down the timber (if too long) or cut a fresh piece (if too short).

As with a normal frame, put two pieces into the corner clamp and adjust until the corners meet precisely. Undo the clamp and remove one piece. Add wood glue to one of the angled ends and replace.

Drill 1–2mm deep pilot holes with the hand drill, or use the bradawl to make an indentation in the wood. Then use the hammer to tap in the panel pins, and the punch and hammer to tap their tops below the surface of the timber.

If you are making a rectangular frame, ensure you clamp together two pieces of differing length – if you attach the two long sides together, or the two short sides together, you will have to undo them as the frame will be impossible to assemble. If your frame is square, it doesn't matter which pieces you glue together first.

When you have made two L-shaped pieces, you can assemble the frame in the same way. You may need to support the back corner of the frame while you do this, using a small pile of books or an object that is the same height as the corner clamp base.

Use wood filler (or glue and sawdust) to fill the holes above the panel pins. Sand these areas, when dry, to a smooth surface.

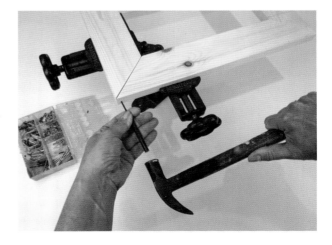

3. While the wood glue and wood filler is drying, you can prepare the 0.1mm soft copper for embossing. Wear gloves to avoid fingermarks.

Measure the width of the frame timber. Use a ruler to mark out this width on the short size of the copper, and mark the line to be cut with a pencil (or an embossing tool).

4. Once you have marked the copper into strips, cut these out by using a pair of old household scissors (this may blunt them slightly).

5. Cut a cardboard offcut to the same width as the strips to make a template for your copper pieces. Turn it 90 degrees and then mark and cut the other side of the cardboard to make a square. Use

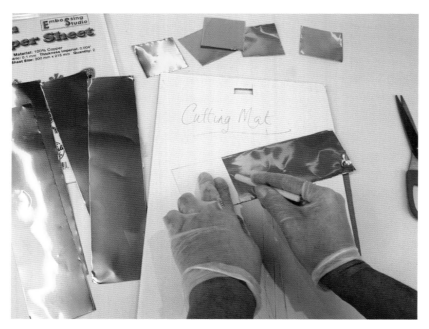

A TURQUOISE TRICK WITH SALT AND AMMONIA.

If you'd like to give your unvarnished copper frame the beautiful and distinctive turquoise patina that forms naturally on pure copper over many years when exposed to damp air, all you need is salt and household ammonia (500ml for approx. £5).

My cousins produced this beautiful verdigris and copper mobile and it showcases the effect of oxidising the lustrous metal.

If you'd like to enhance your frame in this way, make sure to oxidise the copper after you have embossed your copper pieces, but before you attach them to the timber frame.

a. Wash the copper and rinse away the suds. Wear plastic gloves to keep the copper free from fingerprints.

b. Buff the surface thoroughly with 0000 wire wool or fine sandpaper.

c. Sprinkle salt over the surface of the copper – more salt means more verdigris. Go overboard.

d. Lay out the copper pieces in a plastic tray and pour over household ammonia. It's toxic, so make sure you are still wearing gloves. Leave the tray (covered if possible) outside, or in a very well-ventilated area to avoid fumes.

e. After a few hours, the copper pieces will have a beautiful verdigris finish. Lift them out and place them on a clean paper towel to dry, before fitting the copper to the frame following the instructions on page 94.

this template to mark out squares on the strips of copper, using an embossing tool (or old pencil). Cut these out with scissors and lay them out on the frame to check for size.

If you discover a 1–2mm overlap on the edges don't worry as we will deal with that later.

6. It's now time to paint the sides and aperture of the frame with the colour of your choice. I've mixed Mod Podge sealer with copper powder to make a copper glaze. You may prefer to use black enamel paint for contrast, or copper enamel paint.

7. Once you've painted the edges and interior of the frame, leave it to dry by resting it on a few timber offcuts to prevent newspaper sticking to the wet paint. Meanwhile, you can start to emboss your copper squares.

8. Draw freehand images on the copper or cut small pieces of paper to size and draw a guide outline on those. Then take the paper

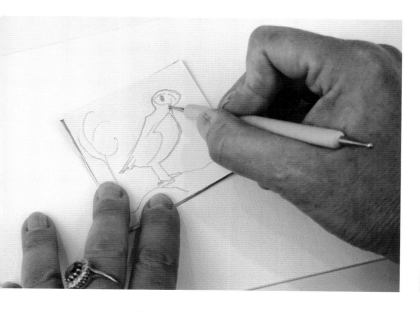
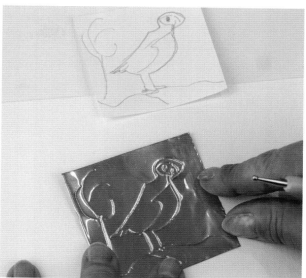

image and emboss it on to the copper by pressing down on the lines with the embossing tool (or an old biro or pencil).

9. Remove the paper to see your transferred outline. It is now time to work into the image using whatever hand tools you like. Anything that makes a mark is suitable. Ideas include cocktail sticks, needles to scratch very delicate lines, lolly sticks to block out larger areas.

NB: *I forgot my gloves in this image and buffed off my fingerprints with lemon juice!*

10. Once you have enhanced your image with more detail, on the front of the copper square, flip it over to add detail from the back – this has the effect of producing raised areas on the front of the image – which is what you are seeking.

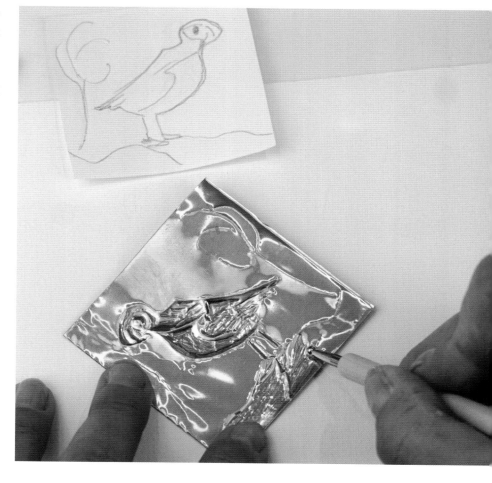

One of the most effective ways of embossing copper is to draw around the lines you have already marked, on the other side of the copper. This will cause the line to 'pop' out further from the surface of the metal.

The same applies to outlined areas: If you 'colour' them in on the reverse repeatedly, they will be gradually raised into relief on the front of the image.

Copper that is 0.1mm thick can take up to 3–4mm of distortion before it will become so thin that your embossing tool will break through the surface. Practise on off-cuts to see what is possible.

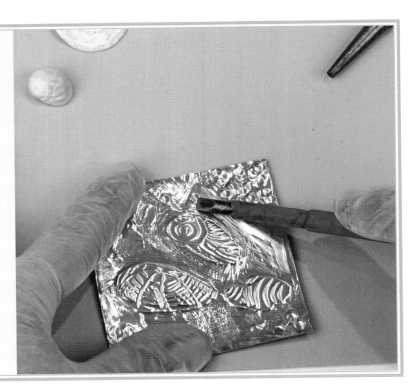

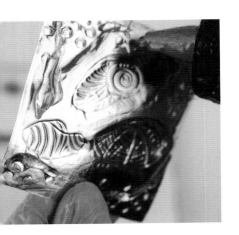

11. Once all your squares are embossed, and the paint on the sides of the frame is dry, it's time to fix them to the timber. Hot glue is effective as it fills some of the cavities on the reverse of the copper, but strong household glue will work well if you weight the copper down carefully with a piece of oversized mount board and some heavy books. If you use hot glue, you will need to work quickly on each piece in turn as it dries fast. Any overspill can be removed with a Stanley knife once all the copper pieces are in position.

12. If you are using hot glue, burnish the edges with a timber offcut after you have applied each piece – especially if they are a couple of millimetres too large. Rubbing the edges of the copper over the lip of the frame gives a neat finish with no sharp edges. If you are using household glue, wait until all pieces have adhered well before doing this.

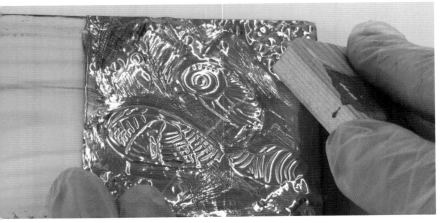

13. If you leave the surface of the frame unvarnished it will eventually begin to oxidise and lose its 'new copper' sheen. If you'd like to preserve this

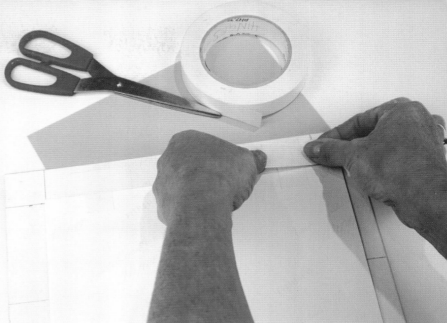

vibrant colour then now is the time to apply two coats of decorator's varnish with a paintbrush.

14. Because your embossed frame has no rebate, you will need to attach your image to the back of the frame directly. If you are using a mount, cut this a few centimetres larger than the aperture in the frame and follow the instructions on pages 30-32 for cutting an aperture in mount board.

When complete, attach your holiday photograph to the back of the mount board with masking tape or acid-free tape.

15. Cut a piece of Art Bak to the same dimensions as the mount – I'm re-using the trimmed board from an old frame in my example. If you wish to make your frame more durable, you will also need a piece of glass the same size.

Make up a 'sandwich' with the layers in this order: glass, mount, image, Art Bak board. Lay it on the frame and check from the front that the mount board is centred within the aperture.

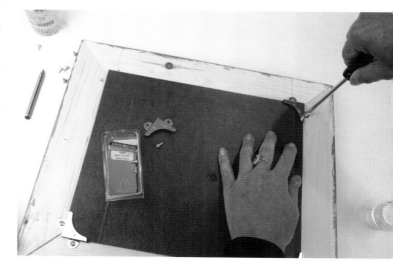

Use a pencil to mark the position of the mirror fixings, which can be bought in a pack of four from any hardware shop. Make pilot holes with the hand drill or bradawl, and use small wood screws to attach the mirror fixings to the timber. Take care not to screw too close to the glass as this can risk chipping it.

Complete your frame with D-rings and picture framing cord, following the instructions on page 42 steps 19 and 20.

Your holiday frame is complete!

CHAPTER SEVEN

60-MINUTE PLANK MIRROR

MIRRORS IN SHOPS often seem overpriced for something so easy to make: four pieces of wood, mirrored glass and fixings.

Follow these simple instructions to make your own DIY version using an old plank. If you want to make a full length mirror, you may need two planks.

I made both these variations – including one with an inbuilt shelf – from a single £10 'gravel board'. These are sold by fencing suppliers and used at the bottom of fences to stop shingle or gravel migrating under the fence. They are a good source of affordable timber.

Alternative timbers include a chunky scaffolding board, reclaimed decking board or a piece of new planed pine.

Making the frame is straightforward, and you can leave it unfinished or paint it any way you wish before you fit the glass – I've suggested two finishes, below.

Mirror glass can be cut to size at your local trade glass supplier; better still trawl charity shops for a mirror you can upcycle. Or give one of your own mirrors a brand new look by removing it carefully from an existing frame.

Equipment
- Tape measure
- A mitre saw or hand saw
- Hand drill with 2–3mm drill bit
- Screwdriver
- Sandpaper
- Paint brush

Ingredients
For flat mirror frame:
- A flat timber plank. To calculate the minimum length of the plank, add the length of one side of the mirror to the length of the top of the mirror and multiply by three. For example: a 30cm x 50cm mirror will require a plank at least 2.4 metres long, i.e. 30cm + 50cm = 80cm x 3 = 240cm.
- A piece of mirror glass – some discolouration on the silvered back can offer an appealing vintage look, as in my turquoise shelf variation.
- Strong wood glue
- Four corner brackets (for a smart touch you could paint chrome ones with gold enamel paint before fixing, as I have done).
- ¾in wood screws
- Pack of four mirror fixings
- Strong picture frame fixings x 2 (use hanging straps for a larger frame or D-rings for a smaller frame)
- Small amount of paint or Danish oil, if required

For shelf variation:
- Four timber screws approx. 5cm long

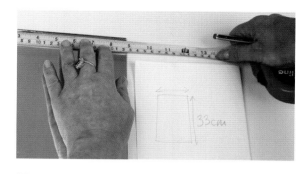

Method:

1. Measure the mirror you wish to use. In this case, 22cm x 33cm.

   Reduce these dimensions by two centimetres.

   For example, 22cm – 2cm = 20cm and 33cm – 2cm = 31cm.

2. Cut two pieces of wood for both top and sides (in this case, two pieces with an internal measurement of 20cm and two pieces with an internal measurement of 31cm). Cut using either a mitre saw or a hand saw (see Insider Tip below). Alternatively, ask your local saw mill or joinery shop if they will cut the timber angles for you. This will take about two minutes on their machinery.

3. Sand the cut edges.

INSIDER TIP:

If the timber you are using is too wide for your mitre saw, you can use a hand saw to measure and cut a 45-degree angle. The handle on the majority of hand saws is manufactured like a set square that helps you mark up both a 90-degree and a 45-degree angle.
To mark a 45-degree angle, place the handsaw at an oblique angle across the plank and press the hilt of the handle up against the timber. The saw blade will now be resting on the wood on the diagonal. Use a pencil to mark a line along the flat side of the blade.

(Whenever you need to cut a 90-degree right angle with a saw, you can do the same by pushing the hilt of the handle straight on to the wood before marking up your straight cut mark with a pencil.)

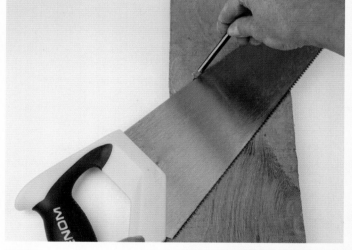

INSIDER TIP:
To use a hand saw to make a diagonal cut in wood, place the timber on a flat surface and angle it diagonally so the cut you are preparing to make with the hand saw will be straight ahead of you and parallel with the edge of the work surface. It's impossible to cut a diagonal line, and it certainly won't be a vertical if you do manage it.

As you saw, concentrate on making a true vertical cut down through the pencil mark at the same time as following it horizontally. If you skew off to one side, your frame may not have square corners.

4. Take a short piece of cut timber in your left hand and a long piece of the cut timber in your right hand, and lay them on your work surface so they make a 90-degree corner. Don't worry if the cuts are not perfectly aligned. You will still be able to secure them with the corner brackets, although the result will be just that little bit more rustic.

Lift the right-hand piece of timber and glue the cut edge with a bead of wood glue then firmly press the two pieces together so the timber can begin to bond (don't worry if they don't touch all the way along).

5. Place a corner bracket about 1.5cm away from the edges of both pieces of wood. Make a pencil mark inside the holes on one side and drill 2mm pilot holes. Fix with short ¾in timber screws (but check first that they won't pierce through your chosen timber). Mark up and pilot drill the other fixings, before screwing the remaining screws into position.

6. Weight down the first corner while you repeat this process on the other two pieces of wood – remembering to keep the short piece of cut timber in your left hand and the long piece of timber in your right hand. Fast-drying wood adhesive will make a good bond in less than ten minutes giving you time to work on the second corner.

7. When both corners are dry, join them together by forming the frame shape and fixing in the same manner with wood glue, followed by the corner brackets.

8. If you wish to oil your mirror to protect and enhance the natural grain of the wood, now is the time. Alternatively, you can paint it using the instructions in the sidebar on page 105.

For an oil finish, take a wad of lint free cotton (such as an old sock or rag) and pour a generous amount of oil on to the mirror, rubbing the oil well into the grain. Remember to do the outside and inside edges as well. You will see the grain in the timber intensify and bring out natural honey tones. Depending how dry the plank is, you may need two coats of oil. Wait for the first to dry for ten minutes before you apply the second.

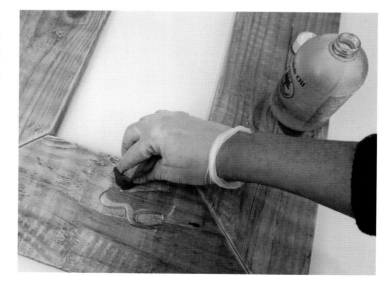

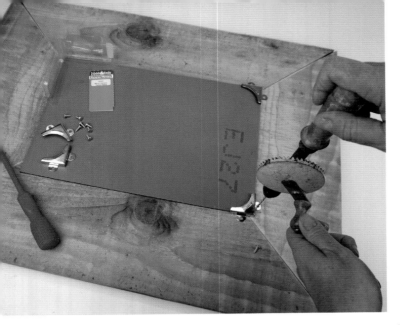

9. Flip your frame over, and place the mirror on it so that its back is facing you. Centre the mirror over the aperture. Mark the position of the first two mirror fixings with a pencil, drill a pilot hole and screw in the supplied screws. It is best to leave a 1mm gap between the edge of the fixing and the mirror to avoid cracking or chipping the mirror. Slide in the mirror to the first two fixings, and fit the second two.

If the mirror seems too loose in the mirror fixings, cut a piece of Art Bak or mount board the same size as the mirror glass and slide it in before fitting the second two mirror fixings. (Remember that if you use cardboard, the mirror will then be suitable only for indoor use in dry areas.)

10. Mark, drill and screw D-rings to the upper edge of the mirror frame so that it can hang vertically in position when fixed to a wall, unlike a framed picture which always has a slight forward angle due to the use of picture framing cord. NB: If the frame is full length you will need to use hanging strap fixings instead and longer screws.

Your 60-minute plank mirror is complete!

For the shelf variation:

12. To make a mirror with built-in shelf, you can either add the shelf to the bottom of the completed mirror frame, or substitute the bottom piece of frame for a shelf – this approach has the added advantage that it requires fewer diagonal corners to be cut!

To make up a three-sided frame, you will need to cut four pieces as timber as shown. The internal measurements should be the same length as the dimensions of your mirror – less 2cm on both dimensions. For example, if your mirror measures 22cm x 33cm, the internal dimensions of the frame pieces should be respectively 20cm and 31cm.

The top piece of the frame should be angled with opposing 45-degree angles on both ends – as in the flat mirror. However, while the two side pieces should still be angled at the tops, the other end of both of them should be cut flat at a 90-degree angle.

Assemble the two top corners of the mirror using glue and brackets (as detailed in steps 3–5 above – remembering to fit the two long pieces either side of the short piece in this instance.)

To make the shelf, measure the width of the frame and cut a length of plank to this length.

13. Add some wood glue to the two ends of the shelf that will connect with the side planks. Press into position, ensuring that the corners where the shelf joins the frame are flush with the sides of the shelf.

14. When the glue is dry, gently mark up and drill pilot holes for the 90-degree brackets to be fitted to both sides of the shelf and the sides of the frame. Screw these into position using your screwdriver.

15. If you intend to use the shelf for anything other than a few toothbrushes – or if there is a bit of gap where the frame sides join the shelf – it's a good idea to give the frame added rigidity by screwing a couple of wood screws into the base of the shelf where it meets the sides of the frame. Mark up and drill pilot holes, then add the screws with a drill or screwdriver – taking care to ensure that the screws will disappear into the bottom of the frame sides and won't be visible.

16. It is now time to fit the mirror and fixings, following the instructions in steps 9 and 10, above. When you fit the mirror fixings, fit the two at the bottom of the mirror first. To do this, place the mirror at the edge of your work-surface so the shelf overhangs. Then fit the mirror fixings low enough to ensure there is no gap between mirror and shelf. Slide in the mirror, and then fit the top two mirror fixings.

If you'd like to paint your mirror, rather than leave it unfinished or oiled with Danish or linseed oil, follow these instructions for a rustic painted finish.

Use a small amount of emulsion on a large dry paintbrush. Smudge the paint into the surface and sides of your plank frame, leaving plenty of gaps in the paint. I've chosen a vibrant turquoise colour to contrast with the honey colour of the wood.

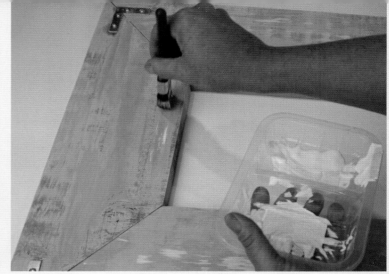

When the paint is dry, apply a second, off-white top coat. Here, I've mixed a tiny a tiny drop of turquoise paint with a teaspoon of white emulsion. Use the top coat very sparingly, to highlight areas by adding a few streaks, here and there, in artistic fashion.

When the paint is dry, rub wire wool firmly over the painted areas to visually soften and age the paint you have applied. In some areas, you might also choose to sandpaper-off the paint down to the bare wood.

To complete the rustic aged effect, rub a thin coat of Danish or linseed oil across the frame, not forgetting the interior and exterior edges.

CHAPTER EIGHT

SHADOW BOX FOR A THREE-DIMENSIONAL OBJECT

SHADOW BOXES – OR MEMORY BOXES – are very deep box frames (deep enough to cast a shadow, hence the name) that allow you to display a three-dimensional item or treasured collection in a way that keeps dust out. They can be custom-made to showcase the precise dimensions of your collection or object, and allow you to draw together images and memorabilia in a stunning wall-mounted display that you can enjoy every day. They are the perfect way to remember a significant moment, place or person in your life.

I've chosen to gather together photographs and objects that remind me of my father Michael, a keen pianist, and his relationship with his sister, Rosemary. Over the years, my aunt has given me small items that belonged to her brother, or that he gave to her, such as decorated handkerchiefs from his travels and even a vintage leather luggage label.

I've also included a photograph of his baby-grand piano; a letter to my mother; the music he loved to play and which I most strongly associate with him; and a photo of me watching him play the piano when I was a toddler.

As I gathered all these items together, and was looking through his piano stool, a note dropped out of the upholstered seat that I had never seen before. It states the date that the seat was first upholstered by him and his father, and the date when he and my mother re-upholstered it. Underneath is a note in his handwriting that says: 'Jane is 19½ months old'. In the search for items for my frame I was able to find this new document, exactly forty years after he died. This project has truly become a memory box to cherish.

IDEAS FOR INSPIRATION: FRAMING A BEACH

I was asked to create this memory box to capture a client's summer wedding and decided to place a real beach inside her memory box, together with bunting and special treasures (I dried the sand in my cooker for an hour to ensure no real moisture would enter the frame).

I fixed Alice-bands worn by bride and bridesmaid into a concealed shelf beneath the sand, using a couple of screws, and inserted several hooks in the ceiling of the frame for bunting and a wooden heart keep-sake.

Five years later, the bride says it is one of her most treasured possessions and she looks at it every day.

In considering ideas for your frame, think about a special event in your life, or a person who you would like to capture in this way – perhaps a parent or sibling, a special journey you've made, keepsakes from your children's childhoods, or a special event.

Memory boxes can be made to any depth and dimension. The only real limitation is the depth of timber you are able to cut on your mitre saw – approximately 7 inches on mine. At that point, the cutting blade is no longer held in position by the retaining arms. If you have access to a table or bench saw, these can be made even deeper.

Equipment
- Tape measure
- A mitre saw or hand saw
- Corner clamp
- Hand drill with 2–3mm drill bit
- Screwdriver
- Sandpaper
- Paint brush
- Wood clamps
- Hammer
- Sandpaper
- Metal ruler
- Stanley knife
- Paint brush (a sash brush is good)
- Wire wool
- Heavy duty picture frame hanging straps x 2
- Optional: Hot glue gun if framing objects too large to be fixed with foam decoupage self-adhesive pads.

Ingredients

- An object or collection you would like to frame, including photographs and/or letters/cards.
- Two pieces of flat timber for the frame (for measurements, see below)
- Planed timber (approx. 5–7mm in depth) to make internal spacers to hold the backing board and Art Bak board (for measurements, see below)
- Art Bak board
- Mount board to be used as backing board
- Foam decoupage self-adhesive pads
- Glass cut to size of rebate
- Wood glue
- Panel pins
- Wood filler
- Paint
- Tube of silicone or strong household glue
- Brown self-adhesive framing tape
- Optional: Gold dust and varnish or Mod Podge
- Hanging straps x 2 and screws

Method:

Firstly, decide the size of your frame so you can buy sufficient timber. To calculate this, gather together a selection of items that you might wish to include and

IDEAS FOR INSPIRATION: PERSIAN SHADOW BOX

I designed this very large display case to look like a fanciful and theatrical museum display case after a friend asked for ideas to display this antique Persian jacket, a treasured heirloom from her husband's side of the family.

The finished frame is 7 inches deep. I hand-tinted the interior and exterior paint colours to match those in the textile, and the exterior was painted in a dark blue, which I oiled slightly to give a fairly flat finish that would contrast with the shimmering fabric inside.

I fitted an internal hanging rail and painted it gold, like the hanger, to enhance the opulence of the piece.

lay them out on your work surface in a tight montage with plenty of overlapping – I was originally going to include the little glass bowls that my father bought on his travels but decided against this as I love them too much to encase them!

When you have a fairly tight arrangement you like, measure from side to side, and top to bottom. Make a note of these measurements.

To calculate the amount of wood you need for your chosen frame size, add the length of all four sides together plus a further 30 per cent to allow for the wastage caused by cutting mitred angles.

You will need two pieces of timber of this length: one will form the front of the frame; the other will become the sides that give depth to your frame.

The front piece of timber should be slightly narrower and thinner than the sides, but will be fixed flat to create a rebate.

For example, for the front of my memory frame I've used timber that is 4cm x 2cm wide. For the sides, I chose a piece measuring 7cm x 2cm.

When these are glued together, it creates a DIY moulding which is 9cm deep (7cm + 2cm). Internally, there is a rebate of 2cm, as well as a usable internal depth of 7cm for the objects, mount and Art Bak.

You will also need to buy a third piece of timber to make four internal spacers that will act as a concealed second rebate (used to hold mount and Art Bak into position at the rear of the frame). Buy a piece of timber that equals

INSIDER TIP:
A memory box looks most effective when items are mounted on different angles. Another trick is for a couple of photographs or documents to 'disappear' out of the frame – you can crop these edges with a Stanley knife in due course (obviously, don't cut off anything crucial that you might need at a later date). These visual tricks create a sense of movement and apparent 'randomness' to the arrangement. You can also roll documents up and tie with ribbon or twine, as I did in the wedding memory frame.

These can be fixed into position using decoupage adhesive foam pads. Bunting looks good and you can also use document pins to fix fabric items, as I've done with the souvenir 1960s handkerchiefs in my memory frame. Small objects such as shells or costume jewellery can be superglued or hot glued together, as with this tiny treasure chest.

the combined length of all four sides, as above, but for this piece you will need only 10 per cent for wastage as you will square cut, not mitre cut, the ends. Narrow timber that is fairly wide is good, but it must be at least 1cm narrower than the timber chosen for the sides of the frame. For my spacer, I chose timber that was 9mm x 6cm wide – chosen because the sides of my frame measure 7cm.

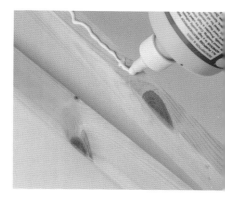

2. To make your DIY moulding, take the two longer pieces of wood and apply glue all the way along the narrow side of the bigger piece of timber – this will form the sides of the frame.

Bond it to the back of the wood that will form the front of the frame, ensuring that one side of the lower timber is flush with the outside edge of the top timber – this will automatically create a single overhanging lip, or rebate, on the other side.

3. Add pressure while the glue dries, with small clamps or strips of masking tape wound tightly around the bonded timber in five or six locations. Take care to ensure that the outside edge of the lower timber remains flush with the outside edge of the top timber while you do this.

Creating a flat bonded join is crucial to the look of the frame (although wood filler and sandpaper will hide a multitude of framing sins if you really become unstuck).

If the timber insists on moving around on the damp glue, you could tap in panel pins in a few locations to secure it – you will remove the pins later, so don't tap them in too far.

4. Once the timber is fully bonded (refer to the glue bottle) you can cut your DIY moulding into the four pieces that you need for your frame.

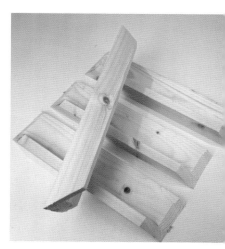

Use the measurements you wrote down in Step 1, above, to cut the timber to size. You need to make sure the top and bottom are the same length, and that the sides match one another.

Ensure that the rebate (the overhanging lip) is facing you when you put the moulding on the mitre saw. For full instructions on how to cut your DIY mouldings, follow steps 7 to 9 in Chapter 5 on page 81.

If the moulding is slightly too tall to be cut by mitre saw, you can use a hand saw. Do so by following the Insider Tip and Sidebar in Chapter 7 on Page 99.

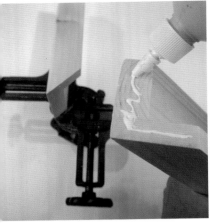

5. Sand all cut ends and then assemble the first frame corner by taking a longer moulding in your left hand and a shorter one in your right hand (if you've made a square frame these will all be the same length, so it won't matter which ones you assemble first). Insert these two pieces into the corner frame clamp so they make a perfect right angle. Apply glue to the right-hand piece and clamp into position.

6. Drill shallow pilot holes with a 1–2mm drill bit so that the panel pins won't split the timber. Tap them in with the hammer, and then use the punch and hammer to tap the tops of the panel pins 1 or 2 millimetres beneath the surface of the timber. For more detail, see directions on page 37.

7. Make up the second L-shaped frame piece. Then, attach both L-shaped pieces together to form the frame, supporting the back corner with an object or small pile of books while you work on the front corner.

8. Fill the holes above the panel pins with filler, or wood glue and sawdust. Use shop-bought wood filler to fill any really large gaps. This is likely to be necessary with a frame of this size, so see the Insider Tip on page 82 for more detailed information on how to do this.

9. Sand off excess filler when dry.

10. Make the internal spacers that will hold your mount and Art Bak into position at the back of the frame (I'm holding samples of both to check their depth). First, measure the length of two opposing sides of the aperture in the frame. Then use your mitre saw – set to 90 degrees – to cut pieces of the thin timber to these exact

measurements, less 2mm for wiggle room. Slot them into position, so they are flush with the sides of the frame and barely visible from the front.

Repeat with the other sides of the aperture. Bear in mind that the first two spacers will have reduced the size of the aperture on the other sides, so measure carefully. If you cut the third and fourth pieces too long, just cut a bit off.

11. Glue the spacers into position by pressing them against the frame sides within the aperture.

If you have a particularly deep frame and narrow spacers, you will need to pack them out from underneath so they don't slip while drying. This will also ensure that you have sufficient room for the contents of your frame and do not leave too much wasted space behind the Art Bak.

The placement of the spacers will come down to your individual preference and the dimensions of the object/s you are framing. The important thing is to ensure that they are equally spaced from the front of the frame on all four sides so that the mount board can be fitted flush with the front of the frame.

NB: *If you have a very narrow rebate you will need to fit the glass before you fit the spacers, as this might be difficult once they are in position. Follow the instructions at Step 18 if necessary. You'll also need to paint the outside of your frame before fitting glass (see Step 16), in this instance. However, if you have a generous rebate continue with Step 12, below.*

12. Once the spacers are glued into position, place your frame at the corner of a piece of mount board and push the corner into the lower left hand corner on the inside of the frame. Draw a pencil line around the other two sides of the base of the frame where it touches the mount board.

Using a Stanley knife, cut the mount to fit these dimensions. You will then have a mount that fits snugly inside the top of the frame and rests on the tops of the spacers.

Repeat this with a piece of Art Bak board.

13. Use a ruler to measure in from the edges of the mount board by the width of your spacers (in my case 9mm) and add 2mm to this measurement. Now draw a feint pencil line around the inside of the mount (in this case 11mm from the edges). When you lay out your items on the frame, butt them up against this line – anything over this line can be cut off with a Stanley knife before the frame is assembled – such as the black-tie photograph of my father and aunt at the top of the mount.

Lay out your items on the mount. It's a good idea to take a reference photograph of your layout before you move it to help you with the placement.

Use a pack of decoupage self-adhesive foam pads to stick down your items, starting with the ones at the back first. Use plentifully – you don't want things to come unstuck once the frame is assembled.

Stick them away from the edges of the items you are fixing so you don't see them. This has the bonus that it can create appealing additional shadows.

14. Press down firmly on the items to get them to adhere to the layers behind, as with this luggage label. If you are framing larger three-dimensional objects – such as an award or ornament – it's a good idea to use a hot glue gun to ensure they stay in position on the bottom or back of the frame.

INSIDER TIP:

Remember, this isn't a collage or flat decoupage, it's an assemblage of items that look most effective when arranged in a mildly haphazard, apparently unplanned style – rather than in regimented stuck-down rows.

Montages such as this are even more effective when you incorporate a three-dimensional element, such as loose corners.

If you are framing a lot of paper-based items, as I have, use double or treble thickness of sticky mounts to build up depth and cast those appealing shadows across the neighbouring items. Make sure you remove the paper backing on each sticky layer as you assemble a little tower of between two and four of them, or they will soon come unstuck.

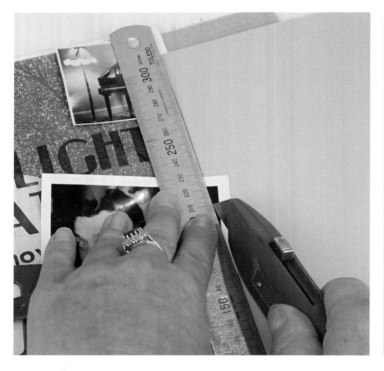

15. When you are happy with the placement of your objects and ephemera, use a metal ruler and a Stanley knife to trim any paperwork that strays beyond the pencil mark on the mount board. Slide a mount board offcut underneath to avoid damaging the mount.

16. You can now paint your frame. My aunt's favourite colour is sapphire blue, so I used two coats of blue emulsion. You could also use enamel paint.

17. If using emulsion, buff with wire wool to create an appealing lustre. When the paint is dry, paint the inside of the frame. I've used an off-white parchment colour for a vintage look. A pale colour such

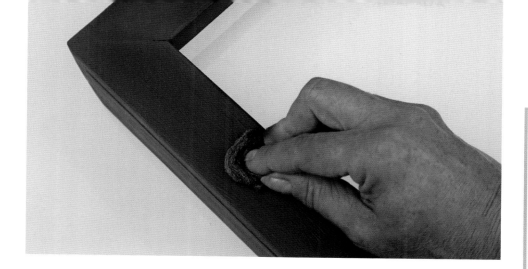

as this also refracts the light in your frame.

I also added a glaze of gold dust with Mod Podge on the front and sides of the frame, applied with a soft sash brush.

INSIDER TIP:
Using a contrasting rich or dark colour on the inside of the frame, such as plum, cerise or gold, can add a sense of drama or mystery to your shadow frame – like peering into an old museum display case or circus dressing room.

18. Fit a piece of clean glass or Perspex to the inside of the frame using silicone or strong household glue. You could also use a hot glue gun. With a shadow box, the glass needs to be stuck into position because there will be no mount board pressing against it from the back of the frame, as with a conventional frame.

The glass should be cut approximately 1cm larger than the aperture in the frame, if the width of the rebate allows this given the depth of the spacers.

19. While the glue dries, place a cardboard offcut on the glass and weigh down with a heavy object to guarantee good adhesion.

20. Carefully clean the inside of the glass, ensuring there is no dust,

INSIDER TIP:
If you end up with silicone or household glue on the front of the glass after you press it down, don't attempt to wipe it off while wet. Wait until it is fully dry and then use a blade from your Stanley knife to cut vertically through the silicone against the side of the frame – taking care not to shave off any paint. You can then angle the blade obliquely and scrape the silicone from the glass in one piece.

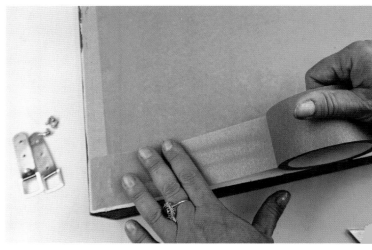
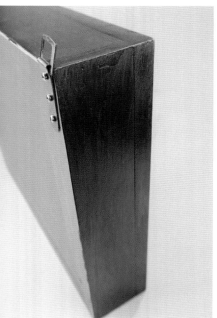

and place your decorated mount board inside the frame so that it rests on the spacers. Add the Art Bak board.

21. Fix the board in position following Steps 17 and 18 on page 42.

22. Attach strap hangers to the rear of the sides of the frame using longer screws. You may need to drill a pilot hole first. Don't support a heavy frame from the top alone.

Your memory box is complete!

APPENDIX: LIST OF SUPPLIERS AND RESOURCES

Buy local when possible

Support your local hardware store, craft shop and independent picture framing shop whenever possible. Picture framers may be happy to discuss ideas with you, and to sell small quantities of materials such as mouldings, mount board and Art Bak board. This will save you having to buy larger quantities online when making your first few frames. Ask if they have any leftover mouldings or mount card you can practise on. Mount boards are also widely available in craft shops.

For planed timber your nearest hardware store will have a good selection. Also, check out your nearest timber or builders' merchant, such as Lakers, Jewson or Travis Perkins. These are usually open to members of the public even if you are buying tiny quantities.

Hardware stores and builders' merchants also sell silicone, glues, wood screws and panel pins etc. They may also stock self-adhesive cork tiles, as well as blackboard paint for the decoupage projects in this book.

eBay.co.uk

Good source for the copper required in Chapter 6. I bought Peak Dale Copper Foil Pack thin 0.1mm 2 sheets (Approx A4) for £7.85 with free postage.

eBay is also a good source for new or second-hand tools, and timber moulding off-cuts. Search for 'Picture frame moulding job lot' to find bargains.

gumtree.com

Classified ad site that can be a good source of tools and timber moulding off-cuts, with the added advantage that you are buying second hand. Search for 'picture frame mouldings'.

craftyarts.co.uk

This hobby site sells the Logan Team System Mat/Mount Cutter – a bevel-edge mount cutter and straight edge which is ideal for the projects in this book. £35 for cutter or £68 for cutter and straight edge.

toolstation.com

Shop here to find the Precision Mitre Saw made by Silverline (approx. £25) and spare 550mm blades. They also sell a basic Corner Clamp for £3.65.

screwfix.com

Shop here for 0000 Liberon Steel Wool for buffing your emulsion finish. Screwfix also sells a Hand Mitre Saw for £29.99 including VAT and a quality Mitre Clamp for £9.99.

framerscorner.co.uk

Manufacturers of professional equipment who now produce a range of DIY products sold in the Hobby Framing section of their website, including the Team System Plus combined mount cutter and straight edge for £48, as well as the T225 Hand Operated Tab Driver for £29.

They also sell the Charnwood PFK03 Picture Frame Assembly Kit for £15 including VAT. This is an ideal starter kit for assembling mitred timber (so you will also need to buy a mitre saw as this is not included). The kit includes a quality adjustable metal corner clamp, magnetic driver for inserting metal V-shaped fasteners to hold the corners together, and a 165-piece hardware kit for finishing and hanging the frame.

Please note, prices may vary but were correct in mid-2021.